AS Psychology
UNIT 1

Edexcel

Cognitive, Social and
Development Processes

Christine Brain

Philip Allan Updates
Market Place
Deddington
Oxfordshire
OX15 0SE

tel: 01869 338652
fax: 01869 337590
e-mail: sales@philipallan.co.uk
www.philipallan.co.uk

ISBN-13: 978-0-86003-884-9
ISBN-10: 0-86003-884-X

This Guide has been written specifically to support students preparing for
the Edexcel AS Psychology Unit 1 examination. The content has been neither
approved nor endorsed by Edexcel and remains the sole responsibility of
the author.

Printed by Information Press, Eynsham, Oxford

P00482

Contents

Introduction

■ ■ ■

Content Guidance

■ ■ ■

Questions and Answers

Introduction

About this guide

This is a guide to Unit 1 of the Edexcel AS specification. Before looking at what this guide is all about, here is some good news (in the form of positive reinforcement). You can pass the exam for this unit, and you can do well. How can I draw this conclusion without knowing you? Because you are reading this guide.

Students who take the trouble to read this sort of guide:
- are motivated to do well
- have an idea about where to look for help
- understand what unit they are taking, and with which examination board
- know something about active learning — we can learn better if we engage in tasks, such as using this sort of student guide

So you already have some of the skills and knowledge you need — hence my claim that you can do well. However, this guide:
- is not a textbook — there is no substitute for reading the required material and taking notes
- does not tell you the actual questions on your paper, or give you the answers!

Aims

The aim of this guide is to provide you with a clear understanding of the requirements of Unit 1 of the AS specification and to advise you on how best to meet these requirements.

This guide will look at:
- the psychology you need to know about
- what you need to be able to do and what skills you need
- how you could go about learning the necessary material
- what is being examined
- what you should expect in the examination
- how you could tackle the different styles of exam question
- the format of the exam, including what questions might look like
- how questions are marked, including examples of answers, with examiner's comments

How to use this guide

A good way to use this guide is to read it through in the order in which it is presented. Alternatively, you can consider each topic in the Content Guidance section, and then turn to the relevant question in the Question and Answer section. Whichever way you use the guide, try some of the questions yourself to test your learning. Hopefully, you will know enough about the marking by this time to try to grade your own answers. If you are working with someone else, mark each other's answers.

The more you work on what is needed, the better. Have your textbooks available too — you will need access to all the relevant information.

Study skills and revision strategies

If you have been studying the Unit 1 material, and have engaged in a reasonable amount of learning up to now, you can make good use of this guide.

This guide can also help if you know very little of the material and have only a short time before the examination. If this describes you, you have a lot of work and long hours of study ahead — but you can do it.

Before reading on, answer the following questions:
- How long is left before the exam?
- Do you have a revision plan?
- Are you sure you want to pass, and hopefully do well? Renewing your motivation can help.
- Are you stressed and in a panic?
- Can you stick to your plan, and trust it?

If you need to, draw up a revision plan now, remind yourself that you want to succeed, and practise some relaxation techniques.

How to learn the material
- Make notes, but be concise and use your own notes for final revision.
- Have a separate sheet of paper for each approach.
- For each approach, note down the six headings (see the summary at the end of each approach) and use that as a guide. Leave room to fit your notes in under each heading.
- Read through each section, then make notes as needed (very briefly).
- Be sure to make notes on evaluation points.
- Finally, note down briefly three things about a contemporary issue that describe the issue, and six 'facts' linking concepts to the issue.

Another useful method is to use cards for each topic. Have the topic heading on one side of the card and brief notes on the other. Remember to note down equal amounts of knowledge and evaluation.

Revision plan

- Start at least 4 weeks before the exam date (sooner if possible).
- Using times that suit you (6 a.m. might be a great time to study!), draw up a blank timetable for each of the weeks.
- On the timetable, fill in all your urgent commitments (cancel as many plans as you can).
- Divide up what is left, allocating slots to all your subjects as appropriate. Don't forget to build in meal times, breaks and time for sleep.
- Stick to the plan if at all possible, but if you have to, amend it as you go.
- When studying, have frequent, short rests, and no distractions.

Time management

Answer the following questions to see how good you are at time management:

(1) Are you usually punctual?

    yes   no

(2) Do you tend to work fast and then correct mistakes?

    yes   no

(3) Do you often put things off?

    yes   no

(4) Do you feel stressed because you never have enough time?

    yes   no

(5) Do you work slowly and carefully, and try to get things right first time?

    yes   no

(6) Do you daydream?

    yes   no

(7) Are you forgetful?

    yes   no

(8) Do you find it hard to get started?

    yes   no

(9) Do you keep your desk tidy?

    yes   no

Score 0 for 'yes' and 1 for 'no' to questions 1, 5 and 9. Score 1 for 'yes' and 0 for 'no' to questions 2, 3, 4, 6, 7 and 8. A score of 3 or below means quite good time management; a score of 4 and above means you need to work on it.

Relaxation techniques

Boxes 1, 2 and 3 suggest ways to relax. Use these as appropriate.

Box 1: Technique 1 — takes about 10 minutes

This technique is useful at the start or at the end of a longish revision period.

- Sit on the floor and make yourself comfortable.

- Working from toes to head, tense each of your muscles in turn and then relax.

- Having relaxed your body, now relax your thoughts.

- Take yourself in your mind to a place where you feel at peace — this could be a favourite holiday place, or a favourite place on a walk. Closing your eyes will help.

- Have a good look around (mentally!), sit down there and hear the sounds of the place.

- Stay there and try not to come back yet.

- When you are ready, come back. Slowly start to hear the sounds around you, and lie with your body relaxed for a little while longer.

Box 2: Technique 2 — takes about 5 minutes

This technique is useful as you revise. Work for between 30 minutes and an hour, and then stop to relax as follows:

- Sit comfortably and try to ignore anything going on around you.

- Imagine you are in a barn, sitting on the rafters under the roof, swinging your legs and sitting comfortably. Closing your eyes will help.

- Now, imagine that the barn has open doors at both ends, and there is a river rushing through from one end of the barn to the other. You are sitting swinging your legs, watching the river rush through below you.

- Hear the water rushing through, sit comfortably, and just watch.

- Think of the water as your thoughts rushing away.

- You are not involved, just watching.

- After about 3 minutes or when you are ready, slowly start to hear the sounds around you, and gradually bring your thoughts back into the real world. Look around you for a minute or two and check that you feel better, before getting back to work.

Box 3: Technique 3 — takes about 1 minute

This technique is useful when you are actually in the examination, and can be used if you are too anxious to continue.

- Imagine you are in an exam now.

- Imagine that you are getting anxious.

- Pick up a pen as if to write.

- Hold the pen up in front of you and stare at it.

- Let all your other thoughts go and think about the pen.

- Try to think of nothing else even for a few seconds.

- Get back to work!

Examination structure and skills

Unit 1 consists of six main questions, ranging across the three approaches. There are two questions for each approach, although marks are not evenly distributed between the approaches. The aim is to ask questions covering the six areas within the approaches, as well as the three approaches themselves. For example, if you are asked a question about common research methods in the cognitive approach, you are unlikely to be asked a 'method' question for the other approaches. Remember the six main areas: two key assumptions; research methods; in-depth area(s) of study; two studies in detail; one key application and one contemporary issue. The three approaches for Unit 1 are the cognitive approach, the social approach and the cognitive–developmental approach. You need to be prepared to answer a question on any of the six main areas for each of the three approaches.

Each exam paper has reasonably straightforward questions at the start, leading to an extended writing question (essay question) at the end. Don't think that someone sets each paper with past papers in front of them, avoiding what has been asked before. Imagine someone trying to set an interesting paper, covering the six areas, ranging across the approaches, and balancing AO1 and AO2 marks according to the required percentages of each. It is not possible to guess what will be on the paper — don't try. Prepare answers for all possible questions. The only guarantee is that there will be an essay question at the end of each paper, and the mark allocation for that essay will be 10 or 12 marks.

Different people set the papers, and there are not as many strict rules as you might think. Tips in this guide include words such as 'usually'. Each paper will be different, and you have to be prepared to answer whatever questions appear. For example, there are many ways that a table can be presented, and you can be asked to tick state-ments, cross false statements, join correct claims together and so on. Read the question carefully and do what is asked, and you will do well.

Assessment objectives

The assessment objectives are listed in the specification. A brief explanation is given below, but check the full list of what you will be assessed on.

Assessment Objective 1: knowledge and understanding (AO1)

- You need to explain your knowledge and understanding of psychological termi-nology and concepts through appropriate use and application.
- You must demonstrate knowledge and understanding of psychological theories, studies, methods and concepts, as well as psychological principles, perspectives and applications.
- You must communicate clearly and effectively, and present and select material well. For example, if you are asked to give a weakness of experiments and you

say they are not valid, this does not get a mark, as you have not shown any under-standing (although you have shown knowledge). You need to make the point clearly — for example, experiments are not valid as they do not take place in a natural setting. You may lose marks by using bullet points, so avoid them. The problem with bullet points is that they encourage short-hand, meaning that your answer will not be clearly and effectively communicated.

Assessment Objective 2: evaluation and comment (AO2)

You must be able to:

- analyse and evaluate psychological theories and concepts, referring to relevant evidence
- appraise psychological studies and methods

Assessment Objective 3 (AO3)

Assessment Objective 3 is examined in Units 3 and 5, and is not dealt with here.

The Unit 1 exam

Unit 1 is assessed in a 90-minute exam. Answers are written in a booklet similar to those used at GCSE, and you can use spare paper too. 72 marks are available. This means you need to score around 1 mark per minute, with 18 minutes to spare for reading and thinking. In general, you can expect to gain 1 mark for each point that answers the question, or for elaboration of a point. Answers must be communicated 'clearly and effectively' (see AO1 above). Avoid one-word answers unless they are asked for. The final essay question is worth 10 or 12 marks. Overall, approximately 42 marks are awarded for knowledge and understanding (AO1) and 30 marks for evaluation and comment (AO2).

Essay mark scheme

Essay questions are likely to be about a key application or a contemporary issue, but other areas may be tested.

Essays have 2 marks (AO1 marks) available for clarity and communication (use of terms, spelling and ways of expressing points) and 2 marks (AO2 marks) for balance and breadth. In addition, for a 10-mark essay you need to give three AO1 'knowledge and understanding' points and three AO2 'evaluation and comment' points. For a 12-mark essay, four AO1 points, and four AO2 points, are required.

AO1 and AO2: getting it right

You must be sure to answer the question that is set — you should then cover the AO1 and AO2 skills. The key words in the question (called **injunctions**) guide what you need to write. If you answer the question, you will automatically do what is required. Table 1 shows some examples of how AO1 injunctions are used and Table 2 shows examples of AO2 injunctions. Note that it is not so much the word itself (e.g. 'describe') that makes it AO1 or AO2, as the whole question. The figures in brackets suggest the mark allocation you might expect for such a question.

Table 1 Examples of AO1 questions/injunctions

Type of question	What is being asked for
Describe a theory… (4)	Say what something is (a theory in this case). Imagine describing the theory to someone who knows little about the subject.
Identify a theory… (1)	Give enough information so that the examiner can understand what is being referred to. For example, if asked to identify a memory theory, the answer might be 'working memory model'.
Name a theory… (1)	Name either the theory or the psychologist(s). For example, if the question asks for a memory theory, the answer might be Atkinson and Shiffrin's or the two-stage model.
Outline an assumption… (3)	Follow the instructions for 'describe', but remember that this injunction usually requires less detail, and hence carries fewer marks.
Describe a study… (5)	Try to give the aim of the study, the method, the procedure, the results and the conclusion(s).

Table 2 Examples of AO2 questions/injunctions

Type of question	What is being asked for
Outline a strength of… (2)	You are asked to outline something, so the injunction seems to be AO1 (i.e. knowledge and understanding). However, as what is outlined is a *strength* (in this case), and thus you are being asked to evaluate something, this question would carry AO2 marks.
Evaluate a study… (5)	Give comments, criticisms, good points and so on about a study. Consider strengths and weaknesses of the method, perhaps, or criticisms of the ethics involved. Look at alternative findings or consider whether justified conclusions are drawn.
Explain, using cognitive-developmental theory concepts… (6)	Use concepts within cogntive-developmental theory (e.g. scaffolding and discovery learning) to explain something.
Assess the effect of… (4)	Show what the effect of something is (e.g. use of cognitive developmental theory in education) and then suggest to what extent this is useful (assess).

AO1 and AO2: injunctions in essay questions

Essay questions will always involve equal marks for AO1 and AO2. You should demonstrate knowledge and understanding and provide comment and evaluation. Remember spelling and use of terminology (2 AO1 marks for clarity and communication). Remember to address all parts of the question (2 AO2 marks for breadth and balance). Table 3 shows the importance of knowing how AO1 and AO2 marks are split in each examination paper (excluding Unit 3, the coursework element).

Table 3 Approximate mark allocation AO1/AO2

	AO1	AO2	Total
AS Units 1 and 2	42	30	72
A2 Units 4 and 5a*	28	44	72
A2 Unit 6	36	36	72
* Unit 5b has an AO3 (experiment/investigation) component			

Table 3 shows how, for the two AS units, you will be assessed more on your knowledge and understanding (58%) than on your ability to comment and evaluate (42%). However, for two of the A2 units, you will be assessed more on your ability to comment and evaluate (61%) than on your knowledge and understanding (39%). For Unit 6, your knowledge and understanding and your evaluation and comment skills are assessed equally.

Essentially, then, you have to learn the material so that you know and understand it, and then plan some criticisms, comments and evaluation points. As a rule of thumb, be sure to learn or plan as many evaluation and comment points as you learn information points.

Conclusions: use of injunctions and the AO1/AO2 split
Don't just think of a word in the question as being the whole question. For example, 'describe' is an AO1 command, but 'describe a strength...' is an AO2 injunction. 'Discuss' could signal AO2 marks if you are asked to 'discuss the usefulness of...' Because you are considering how useful something is, you are doing more than showing knowledge about it. The best approach is to *answer the question*. If you study and understand the question, all should be well.

Content
Guidance

This section provides an overview of what you need to learn for Unit 1. Remember, you need access to more material than is given here.

An attempt is made to balance presenting knowledge with giving suggestions for evaluation. Remember the rule of thumb — you must prepare equal amounts of AO1 and AO2 material.

Structure of the AS units

Each unit comprises three of the main approaches in psychology. Each approach follows the same format:
- two key assumptions (your choice)
- research methods used (some specified ones)
- in-depth area(s) of study (specified)
- two studies in detail (your choice)
- one key application (specified)
- one contemporary issue (your choice)

Unit 1 covers cognitive, social and cognitive-developmental approaches.

As you can see, for some areas of Unit 1 you can choose what you study. In this section suitable material is presented, but you may well have studied different examples.

The cognitive approach

Two key assumptions

—Computer analogy

We process information just as computers do, and there is input–processing–output. An example is the multi-store or dual process model, where information comes in via a sensory store, is processed in short-term and long-term memory, and recall is the output.

Information processing

We process information cognitively. Thinking, perceiving, using language and memorising are all ways of processing information. We receive information, interpret it, and respond in some way.

Summary

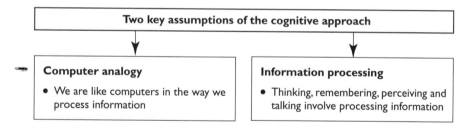

Two key assumptions of the cognitive approach	
Computer analogy	**Information processing**
• We are like computers in the way we process information	• Thinking, remembering, perceiving and talking involve processing information

Research methods used in the cognitive approach

– Laboratory experiments

Experiments take place in controlled conditions, where one variable (the independent variable, IV) is manipulated (changed) in some way to see the effect of this change on another variable (the dependent variable, DV). From this manipulation, a cause-and-effect relationship can often be claimed.

For example, Tulving and Pearlstone (1966) manipulated whether a participant received cues on a recall sheet of paper or wrote their responses on a blank piece of paper. (The IV was whether recall was cued or not; the DV was how many words were recalled.)

Evaluation

+ Variables other than the IV and the DV are tightly controlled, so cause-and-effect conclusions can be drawn. If only the IV changes, and something changes in the DV, we can say that the IV change(s) *caused* the change in the DV. Good controls tend to mean good reliability.
- The IV has to be singled out and all variables controlled. This means that the situation is often very unusual, and only one variable (the IV) is looked at. In real life, things that vary about people are not all separate or measurable in this way. Because of this, experiments are often said to lack validity.

Case studies of brain-damaged patients

Case studies are in-depth studies, often of one person. In cognitive psychology they involve people who have experienced brain damage. Psychologists study what these people can do in terms of processing information, and what they cannot do. They note down what area(s) of the brain are damaged. Then, by seeing what effect the damage has had, they draw conclusions about what that area or those areas are for. The study of HM is an example of a case study of a brain-damaged patient.

Evaluation

+ Real people with real brain damage are studied, so the conclusions drawn have some validity. With modern scanning techniques, many tests can be carried out (with their permission of course). In-depth data can be gathered.
- The damage often involves more than one area, so we cannot really tell which element of damage has what effect. Also, it can be stressful for the participants, who must be able to give full and informed consent.

Summary

Two research methods used in the cognitive approach

Laboratory experiments	Case studies of brain-damaged patients
The IV is manipulated, the DV is measured; other variables are controlled	People with brain damage are studied to see its effect
Advantages	Advantages
• Cause-and-effect relationship is studied	• In-depth information
• Can be repeated (good controls)	• Questions can be asked and a variety of sources of information can be used
• Good reliability	• Real life, so it is valid in a way
	• The damage means the study is not about normal functioning, so to an extent it is not valid
	• Can be repeated, so reliable
Disadvantages	Disadvantages
• Control of variables means it is not real life	• There may be more than one area of damage
• Poor validity	• Can be unethical

In-depth areas of study: two memory theories and two forgetting theories

Memory

Atkinson and Shiffrin's (1968) dual process model

This is an information processing model.

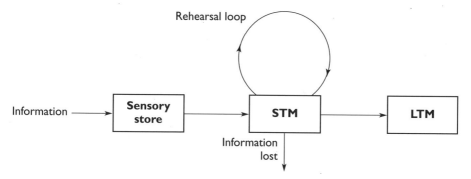

Information enters via the sensory store (via sight, sound, taste, smell or touch), and can then move into short-term memory (STM). If rehearsed, material can be stored in long-term memory (LTM); if not rehearsed, material is lost.

Sensory store

Material enters a sensory store and is stored in the form in which it enters (i.e. sound, sight etc.), but only for a very short time. Information comes in from all around us, but only a small amount survives to reach STM.

Short-term memory (STM)

- Capacity — experiments have suggested that STM holds around 7 ± 2 (between 5 and 9) items (Miller, 1956). However, a 'chunk' can form an item (e.g. the numbers 1–10 can be one item).
- Process — one way of describing how material goes from STM to LTM is to think of a short loop of tape where material is stored for a brief period. As the end of the loop is reached, new material is 'written' over old material, so the amount of material in STM is limited. Material is rehearsed and then stored in LTM; if it is not rehearsed and 'moved' to LTM, it is lost (forgotten).
- Duration — experiments have shown that material lasts in STM for between 18 and 30 seconds before it is either lost or stored in LTM.
- Coding — we tend to repeat material in our heads when rehearsing (e.g. trying to remember a telephone number). It is thought that coding in STM is acoustic (sound).

Long-term memory (LTM)

- Capacity — we have lots of room in long-term memory; its capacity is said to be unlimited.

- Duration — material is potentially never forgotten (lasts) in LTM, although theories of forgetting help shed light on what material is lost, and why.
- Coding — we store material in pictures (visually), in sound, and by using meaning (semantically). We can recall smells too, so it seems that we use different coding in LTM. Meaning seems to be particularly important; adding meaning to material seems to help recall.

Tip

This suggests that organising material and making it meaningful will help you when revising for exams.

Evaluation

+ Evidence supports the model. Glanzer and Cunitz (1966) suggested that early words in a list are often recalled well, and the final words in a list are also recalled, whereas middle material is more likely to be forgotten. They concluded that early words had been moved into LTM, so were recalled. They thought that the late information was still in the STM rehearsal loop, so was recalled easily. Middle material, however, had moved on from STM and was not recorded well in LTM, so it was not recalled easily. This is taken as evidence for the dual process (two-stage) model.

+ Evidence supports the model. Tulving and Pearlstone (1966) (and other later studies) showed that if participants were given cued recall, they recalled more than if they recalled a list freely. Participants learnt words listed in categories. Cued recall meant they were given the category headings to prompt recall, while free recall meant they had a blank piece of paper on which to write the words they remembered. The category headings must have prompted better recall, and this was thought to be evidence that LTM involved meaning.

− One model can be used to evaluate another. If the dual process model is 'believed', then a different model cannot be 'believed'. Another model is the levels of processing (LOP) model, which gives another explanation for how memory works. In evaluating the dual process model, you can restate the LOP model (see below) briefly — explain how this offers another explanation, and suggest that the dual process model is not the only explanation for forgetting.

− There is another model called the working memory (WM) model. This can be said to look more deeply at the working of STM, and to suggest that it is not simply one process. The WM model suggests we have an 'inner voice', an 'inner ear' and an 'inner eye', as well as a means of controlling these sorts of input. This is clearly a more detailed look at the processes involved than is the dual process model; this is a criticism of the STM/LTM model.

➤ Craik and Lockhart's (1972) levels of processing explanation

The levels of processing (LOP) explanation suggests that the main focus should be on information processing, rather than on memory. It is thought that the better the information is processed, the better it is stored and recalled. Memory is a by-product of the processing.

Craik and Lockhart proposed their model based on analysis and ideas, rather than from a direct study. Having proposed the idea, it was then tested by Craik and Tulving, as outlined below when looking at evidence for the model.

Three levels of processing are suggested: shallow, phonemic and semantic. Shallow processing means noting such things as whether a word is in capital letters (to do with seeing). Phonemic processing means noting such things as the sound of a word (to do with hearing). Semantic processing refers to the meaning of things, and means we have some sort of understanding. Recall is best when semantic processing is involved.

Tip

Again, this suggests that your exam revision needs to involve meaning and under-standing, as the dual process model also advocates — so be active in reading this!

Evaluation

+ Evidence supports the model. Craik and Tulving (1975) tested the LOP idea that semantic processing gives better recall. Participants were given a list of words to which they had to respond in various ways. They had to decide if a word was in capital letters (shallow processing), if it rhymed with another given word (phonemic processing), or if it fitted into a sentence (semantic processing). The findings supported the LOP idea, and shallow processing led to least recall, phonemic processing was next best, and semantic processing gave the best recall.
+ The information processing assumption behind cognitive psychology links well with the LOP model, which is all about information processing. We can repeat Craik and Tulving's study easily (and it is well replicated), and find that the deeper processing (where meaning is recalled) leads to the best recall.
− A problem with the LOP explanation of memory is that it is not a real explanation. It simply claims that memory comes from deep processing, and it proves this by showing that memory comes from deep processing. This seems to suggest that deep processing is the same thing as memory, which is perhaps useful but is not really an explanation, just a restatement of what memory (or deep processing) is.
− The dual process explanation may be able to incorporate the LOP explanation. Perhaps rehearsing in STM is the same as deeper processing (by repeating the material in our heads, for example). Chunking improves the capacity of STM, and we could say that chunking involves adding meaning (e.g. noting that 2, 4, 6, 8 is one chunk, because it is the first four even numbers). This is not really arguing against the LOP explanation, but suggesting that it can be incorporated into other models.
− Remember, a model is only a suggested explanation; it needs real evidence (perhaps linking to brain functions) to support it.

Summary

Two theories of memory

Dual process model

Atkinson and Shiffrin (1968)
- Sensory store, STM, LTM
- Rehearsal loop or material lost

For
- Glanzer and Cunitz (1966) — support
- Tulving and Pearlstone (1966) — support

Against
- Other models, such as LOP, can contradict
- Working memory model increases the complexity of STM

Levels of processing

Craik and Lockhart (1972)
- Visual, phonemic and semantic levels
- Semantic is best

For
- Craik and Tulving (1975) — support
- The study is well replicated

Against
- Can be a circular argument
- Evidence fits dual process model too
- Models are only ideas of what happens

Forgetting

Interference: forgetting in STM

According to the Atkinson and Shiffrin model, material has to be rehearsed in STM before being stored in LTM, otherwise it is forgotten. Studies have shown that if there is interference — that is, if this rehearsal is blocked in some way — then less material is transferred to LTM. This is taken as evidence for the STM/LTM model.

Evaluation

+ Evidence backs the claim that interference causes forgetting in STM. The Brown–Peterson technique is a way of showing that interference leads to forgetting in STM. This technique was developed by Brown (1958) and Peterson and Peterson (1959) and involves asking participants to do tasks such as counting backwards aloud, to assess their ability to rehearse material. Those who have their rehearsal blocked by such tasks recall less material than those who can rehearse, and this is taken as evidence for the need for rehearsal. It also means that interference in STM leads to forgetting, thus supporting this explanation of forgetting.

− Although it is easy to replicate the Brown–Peterson style studies, and you can see for yourself that doing tasks such as counting backwards will interfere with your recall, this does not in itself show that interference is blocking some sort of rehearsal loop. Other explanations for forgetting, such as displacement, might explain the forgetting that takes place equally well (new material from the counting might be displacing what the participant is supposed to be recalling). Also, this might not be about STM. The participant might forget what they are asked to recall because they are also focusing on the counting, so the material they are supposed to learn is not so deeply processed — and this focuses on the LOP model, not on STM.

Interference: forgetting in LTM

Interference is also said to cause forgetting in LTM. Proactive interference (called proactive inhibition, PI) is said to occur when learning of old material interferes with learning of new material. For example, you might have learnt the Atkinson and Shiffrin model, then tried to learn about LOP, but information about the first model interfered with (made you forget) learning about the second model, and you could have muddled the two. Retroactive interference (called retroactive inhibition, RI) is the opposite of PI — what you learnt last interfered with (made you forget) what was previously learnt.

> **Evaluation**
>
> + Evidence supports the idea of PI and RI. Studies have shown that if a participant is shown two lists of words and then asked to recall the second list, he/she recalls words from the first list and forgets words from the second list (PI). Similarly, if the participant is shown two word lists and then asked to recall the first list, retroactive inhibition takes place, as words from the second list are recalled, and words from the first list are forgotten.
>
> − In many ways, these studies are about what we remember and not just about what we forget. It means we store information by either focusing on early material (giving PI) or focusing on later material (giving RI). There is interference where one set of material interferes with another set, but it is recall that is muddled, and not just forgetting that is taking place.
>
> − The studies are artificial, and involve participants learning two lists of similar words (or similar tasks); it could be said that this is bound to lead to some sort of interference between the two tasks. If learning two languages at once, we could perhaps have these sorts of problem, but in many tasks we are not trying to learn such similar things at the same time.
>
> − The studies do not give participants much chance to use learning strategies such as adding meaning (as with the LOP model).

Cue-dependent forgetting in LTM

Another reason for forgetting is that we do not have the appropriate cue for recall. Models of memory show that meaningful material is recalled better than material that has no meaning for the person. As we have seen, Tulving and Pearlstone (1966) showed that participants given a cued recall task remember a list of words better than if they have a blank piece of paper for recall. It seems that if we have a cue for something, we recall it better. So it is said that forgetting (lack of recall) can occur if the appropriate cue is not present.

Context-dependent and state-dependent forgetting (Tulving, 1974)

Cues can be about the context or situation in which memories were laid down; absence of these can cause forgetting. This is called context-dependent forgetting. Cues can also be about the state the person is in at the time of laying down the memories; absence of these cues can cause forgetting too. This is called state-dependent forgetting.

Evaluation

+ Studies have demonstrated this type of forgetting, by either adding the cue(s) or not. Participants with the relevant cue(s) recall more than those without the cue(s). This is taken as evidence for cue-dependent forgetting. For example, Godden and Baddeley (1975) used divers, who all learned lists of words when diving. Those who were asked to recall when diving recalled more words than those who were asked to recall in a different context (on the boat or on land). It was thought that cues from the context (or being in similar surroundings) led to this improved recall. Note that the participants who recalled when diving were also in the *state* of diving, not only in the context — the surroundings were familiar to divers, but the state they were in physically was also familiar to them as divers.

− It seems likely that forgetting is caused by not having the right cue to trigger the recall. However, this might not be the cause of all forgetting. There might be other explanations in other circumstances. For example, motivated forgetting suggests that in some circumstances we forget because we do not want to remember. The trace decay theory of forgetting suggests that sometimes we forget because the memory has decayed. Both these explanations might explain some forgetting, while cue-dependent forgetting might explain other types.

− Studies are artificial and tend to be about learning lists of words. This is only one sort of remembering, which reinforces the claim that cue-dependent forgetting might not be a complete explanation.

Summary

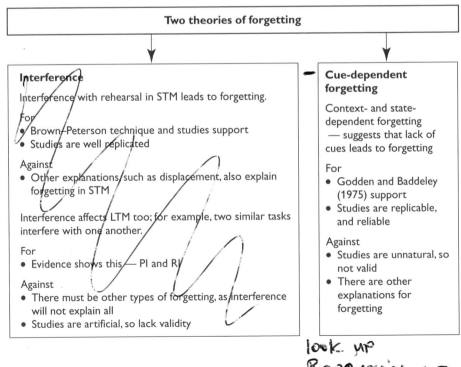

Two theories of forgetting	
Interference Interference with rehearsal in STM leads to forgetting. For • Brown–Peterson technique and studies support • Studies are well replicated Against • Other explanations, such as displacement, also explain forgetting in STM Interference affects LTM too; for example, two similar tasks interfere with one another. For • Evidence shows this — PI and RI Against • There must be other types of forgetting, as interference will not explain all • Studies are artificial, so lack validity	**Cue-dependent forgetting** Context- and state-dependent forgetting — suggests that lack of cues leads to forgetting For • Godden and Baddeley (1975) support • Studies are replicable, and reliable Against • Studies are unnatural, so not valid • There are other explanations for forgetting

look up
Repression p.55

Two studies in detail

━ Leading questions

Loftus and Palmer (1974)

Aim

This looked at the effect of leading questions on participants' answers, to see if the wording of a question can distort the 'recall' (answer) of the participant.

Method

A laboratory experiment was used, with an independent groups design. Different groups were asked different questions (with one change of wording each) to see whether this change of wording (the IV) affected recall in the form of answers given (the DV).

Procedure

Participants were all shown the same film of a car accident. One group was asked to estimate the speed of the cars when they 'hit'. Another group was asked how fast the cars were going when they 'smashed'. Alternative words were used with other groups: for example, 'bumped', 'collided' and 'contacted'. All the groups followed the same procedure except for the change of verb.

Results

Loftus and Palmer found that the stronger the word (e.g. 'smashed' instead of 'hit'), the faster was the estimate of speed. When the word 'smashed' was used, the average estimate of speed was 41 mph, whereas when the word 'contacted' was used, the average estimate of speed was 32 mph.

Conclusion

They concluded that the word used gave some internal image or schema about what was happening, and this also included an element of speed. They concluded that leading questions can affect recall.

The study was extended, and a week later the same participants were asked if they had seen any broken glass. Of those who had been given the word 'smashed', 32% said that they had seen broken glass, but only 14% of those given the word 'hit' recalled broken glass. There was no broken glass shown in the film. This is further evidence that the word used affects recall of the situation. This extra part of the study is also attributed to Loftus and Palmer (1974).

Evaluation

+ As this was a well-controlled experiment, and the only change made between the groups was the word used to describe the accident ('smashed', 'hit', and so on), the study is reliable. If it were done again, the same results would be expected.
+ The study is backed by evidence from other studies. Variations of this study have been carried out with similar results, also showing that leading questions can affect recall.

- Being an experiment, it can be criticised as not being valid. It was not a real accident, but a film of one. There would not have been the tension of a real incident. Also, the participants were not estimating speed for a 'real' reason — it was just a study — so they may not have taken the study seriously.
- Other studies have shown that misinformation can lead to the wrong conclusions being drawn, or wrong recall. However, if the misinformation is obviously incorrect, then participants are much less likely to make an error. The speed of the car was not easy to estimate, so the participants relied on the descriptive word. This is not an unreasonable thing to do, and only means that when other information is not available, people will use what information they have. This does not mean that all leading questions will lead to incorrect testimony.

Levels of processing

Craik and Tulving (1975)

Aim

Craik and Tulving (1975) were testing the levels of processing theory of memory. The LOP model suggests that the deeper the level of processing, the better the recall. There are three levels of processing: visual/structural, phonemic/sound, and semantic/meaning. The first level (structural) should be least well recalled, phonemic processing gives better recall, and the best recall is when semantic processing takes place. The aim of the study was to find evidence for this claim.

Method

A laboratory experiment was set up using a tachistoscope. With this device, words can be flashed in front of a participant (looking down onto a screen), without other distractions. The time between words can be controlled, as can the length of time the word is displayed. A repeated measures design was used and participants were asked questions about the words they saw, each question needing a different level of processing.

Procedure

Participants saw words through a tachistoscope and were asked one of four different types of question about each word:
- whether the word was in capital letters (representing structural or visual processing). The participant only had to look at the word and process its structure.
- whether the word rhymed with another word (representing phonetic or phonemic processing). The participant had to process the sound of the word.
- whether the word was a type of food (representing semantic processing). The participant had to know the meaning of the word and link it to foods.
- whether the word would fit into a sentence like 'he kicked the ____ into the tree' (representing semantic processing). The participant had to consider the meaning of the word, for example when seeing if it fitted into this sentence.

Once the participants had answered 'yes' or 'no' to these questions, they were given a recognition test. They had to say which words they had seen before. The words in the recognition test were the ones they had viewed through the tachistoscope, but there were other words as well. The question was, how many words would the participant recognise, and would they recognise more of the words they had processed semantically than words they had processed in a more shallow way?

Results

The results agreed with the LOP claim that semantic processing leads to better recall. The more deeply processed words were recognised more often.

Conclusion

Craik and Tulving concluded that memory is improved by deeper processing, and that structural processing is the least deep, with phonemic being the next deepest, and semantic processing leading to the best recall.

Evaluation

+ This was a well-controlled experiment and so the results should be reliable. The time the words were viewed for, the questions asked and even participant variables were all controlled. (Participant variables were controlled because the same participants did all the conditions.)
+ The study has been replicated often (including by AS students) and the findings have been repeated, so it can be claimed to be reliable. To add to this claim, consider studies that look at how categories can aid recall in LTM. Categorising can be said to add meaning, adding weight to the claim that semantic processing is best — although this does not necessarily mean that the LOP model is a good explanation of this.
− The task was a recognition task, so we should take care in drawing conclusions about recall. However, it is likely that recall is improved by semantic processing.
− Even if the study shows that semantic processing is best, and it does seem to show this, it does not prove that the LOP explanation is right. The LOP explanation tends to be circular, because on the one hand it says that deep processing is semantic processing and is better recalled, and then on the other hand it takes as proof of this that semantic processing is better recalled.

Summary

Two studies from the cognitive approach

Loftus and Palmer (1974)	Craik and Tulving (1975)
• When asking about the speed of a car, questioners used key words like 'hit' and 'smashed' • Witnesses' recall was affected by these key words	• Semantic processing led to better recall • Words processed by looking at meaning were remembered more often

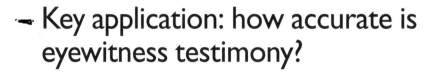

Key application: how accurate is eyewitness testimony?

The key application for the cognitive approach examines issues to do with eyewitness testimony and eyewitness memory. Loftus and Palmer's (1974) study outlined above provides some of the background regarding possible problems with eyewitness memory.

The accuracy of memories of eyewitnesses can be questioned (as can the accuracy of all memory). The table below lists some of the ideas or concepts of the cognitive approach and shows how they can be applied to eyewitness testimony (EWT).

	Issue 1	Explanation 1
Cognitive finding	Memory is reconstructive	We make sense of information and recall it, having reorganised it; Bartlett (1932) used his 'War of the Ghosts' story to demonstrate this
Applied to EWT	Eyewitness memory may be reconstructed	Eyewitnesses will probably reorganise events so that they make sense; therefore, they may not give a 'true' account
	Issue 2	**Explanation 2**
Cognitive finding	Memory is affected by stress	Our physiological make-up affects us in times of stress (e.g. our fight/flight response is activated); this in turn can affect our memory
Applied to EWT	EWT is affected by the level of arousal in the situation, which is likely to be high	The weapons effect has been found (i.e. people may focus on the weapon, if present, and recall fewer of the other factors, so EWT is affected); this in turn can affect our memory
	Issue 3	**Explanation 3**
Cognitive finding	Memory is reconstructive and maybe affected by attributional biases	Attributional bias affects our judgements and attributions (e.g. judgements of who we think is to blame in a situation)
Applied to EWT	EWT can be affected by attributional biases; for example, the fundamental attribution error, self-serving bias and/or hedonic relevance	The fundamental attribution error refers to our tendency to blame (attribute negative cause to) the disposition of other people (e.g. you missed the bus), whereas we blame situational reasons (e.g. the bus was late) for our own behaviour; this can affect EWT

	Issue 4	Explanation 4
Cognitive finding	Memory is reconstructive and can be biased; leading questions can cause bias	A schema is used, and can shape recall — the choice of schema can be shaped by choice of wording
Applied to EWT	EWT can be affected by leading questions	Changing a word from 'the' to 'a' can affect recall; asking about 'the' broken headlight leads to more broken glass being recalled than asking about 'a' broken headlight

How to overcome bias in EWT

Reconstructing the setting

When witnesses reconstruct memories, they need to have the original setting recreated as far as possible. We draw on a schema to help in recall, and a setting is a powerful part of a schema. So if the setting is reconstructed, the reconstructed memory is more likely to draw on an accurate schema.

Cognitive interviews

Cognitive interviews aim to reconstruct not only the setting but other cues too, such as feelings at the time and cognitions such as thoughts and plans at the time. This technique tries to ensure that reconstruction rests on a 'real' schema.

Evaluation

– Much evidence about bias in EWT comes from laboratory studies, which can be said to be unnatural situations, so they lack validity. For example, tensions from a 'real' crime would not be represented.
– Problems with EWT are just some of the difficulties faced when trying to prove guilt in a crime. Other factors, such as the characteristics of the defendant, are also involved.

Summary

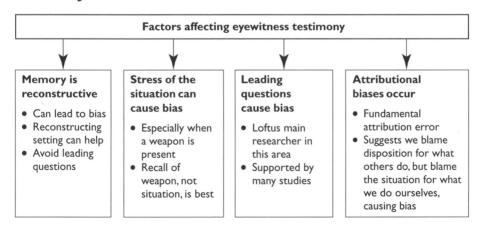

Factors affecting eyewitness testimony

Memory is reconstructive
- Can lead to bias
- Reconstructing setting can help
- Avoid leading questions

Stress of the situation can cause bias
- Especially when a weapon is present
- Recall of weapon, not situation, is best

Leading questions cause bias
- Loftus main researcher in this area
- Supported by many studies

Attributional biases occur
- Fundamental attribution error
- Suggests we blame disposition for what others do, but blame the situation for what we do ourselves, causing bias

Contemporary issue

In the cognitive approach, you can adapt the key application as a contemporary issue if you wish, and this means that you will have less material to learn. However, you may have studied a different contemporary issue.

Problems with EWT: injustice?

Psychologists have raised issues about the accuracy of EWT as used in court and by the police. In court, EWT can be challenged on the basis of probable biases. The police can try to ensure that eyewitness evidence is accurate and unbiased by using cognitive interviews, which go some way towards gathering evidence in a more accurate way. It is important for the police to try to get as accurate a picture as possible, and it is important for defendants that they get a fair trial, with unbiased witnesses if possible.

Summarising the issue
- EWT is likely to be biased.
- The police need unbiased testimony.
- Defendants need unbiased testimony.

EWT: concepts in cognitive psychology

Elizabeth Loftus has done many studies showing bias in EWT. Loftus and Palmer (1974) (outlined on pages 23–24) showed that judgement of speed is affected by leading questions, such as asking about cars that 'smashed' into one another or 'hit' one another. The former leads to higher estimates of speed. So the words asked in a trial or by police interviewers could affect EWT.

Witnesses' own biases can affect EWT too. For example, the fundamental attribution error can lead a witness to blame another person (e.g. 'the driver was speeding'), whereas he or she may not equally blame themselves (e.g. 'the road was wet').

Cognitive interviews can help to achieve accurate EWT when the witness is mentally 'taken back' to the situation to set an accurate scene, rather than allowing free reconstruction. Sometimes, a real reconstruction takes place, so that a witness is both mentally and physically taken back to the situation. This tends to create accurate schema, and can avoid a reconstruction that draws more on imagination and which may be inaccurate. *look up Recovered memories P.63*

Summary of the cognitive approach

- **Two key assumptions**: 'the computer analogy' and information processing
- **Research methods**: laboratory experiments and case studies of brain-damaged patients

- **In-depth areas of study**: two theories of memory, for example the dual process and LOP, and two theories of forgetting, for example interference and cue-dependent forgetting
- **Two studies in detail**: for example Loftus and Palmer (1974) and Craik and Tulving (1975)
- **Key application**: bias in eyewitness testimony
- **A contemporary issue**: for example problems with eyewitness testimony

The social approach

Two key assumptions

Culture and society

We are affected by our culture and society, which help to shape our behaviour. We do not act separately as individuals so much as within a social setting. For example, our culture affects our view of what we think of as mental illness. In one culture, hearing voices may be seen as a spiritual gift, to be respected, whereas in another it would lead to a diagnosis of schizophrenia.

Social roles

We are affected by how others see us and by the roles we are allocated. We don't just carry out actions — we interact. One example of how we are affected by others is the self-fulfilling prophecy. Others can label us, and then through a self-fulfilling prophecy we might fulfil that label. We fulfil roles allocated to us too, and behave according to them. Haney et al. (1966) (the Zimbardo study) found that when randomly allocated the role of a guard, an individual acted as he thought a guard would. If given a role, we are likely to fulfil expectations attached to that role.

Summary

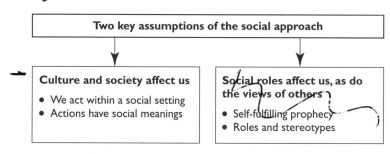

Two key assumptions of the social approach

Culture and society affect us
- We act within a social setting
- Actions have social meanings

Social roles affect us, as do the views of others
- Self-fulfilling prophecy
- Roles and stereotypes

Research methods used in the social approach

— Field experiments

Field experiments have many of the characteristics of laboratory experiments, but instead of taking place in a laboratory, they take place 'in the field' (for example, in the participants' natural setting).

As with laboratory experiments, there is strict control of variables, the IV is manipulated and the DV is measured. If all variables except the IV are controlled for, we can say the changes in the IV *cause* any changes in the DV.

Field and laboratory experiments include standardised instructions (also as a control). Efforts are made to avoid sources of bias, such as experimenter bias and demand characteristics. These efforts include single-blind techniques (in which the participants are not aware of the purpose of the study) and double-blind techniques (in which neither the participants nor the experimenter are aware of the purpose of the study).

Field experiments are not naturalistic experiments. They involve manipulating an IV just like laboratory experiments. Naturalistic experiments, on the other hand, involve studying a naturally occurring IV, where manipulation is not needed and what is required occurs naturally. An example of a field study is Hofling et al. (1966).

Evaluation

+ Field experiments use a natural setting in some way, and are less artificial than laboratory experiments. They have greater validity, as they are more likely to be looking at 'real-life' (natural) behaviour or events.
+ Field experiments have the same advantages as laboratory experiments. Good controls tend to mean that a study is replicable. The study can be repeated if the procedure is clear, and reliability is therefore likely to be good.
− Although done in a natural setting, these are still experiments. Controls are likely to mean that some of the procedure at least is not natural, so although validity is better than in laboratory experiments it can still be criticised. Ecological validity may be gained, as the setting is natural, but validity regarding the task may be criticised.
− Control of variables is more difficult in a field setting than in a laboratory because external factors are harder to manipulate. For example, weather conditions, noise levels, heat and light can vary, while interruptions by others can occur.

— Surveys

Surveys can include questionnaires and structured interviews. Questionnaires involve asking all participants a set list of questions. These questions are often closed, meaning there is a set choice of answers, and the participant cannot add anything. This helps when comparing answers. Questionnaires can also include some open questions. These allow the participant to give views and comments.

Closed questions yield **quantitative data** (the numbers of 'yes' and 'no' answers, for example, can be added up and compared, emphasising quantity of answers). Quantitative data are easier to analyse in many ways because participants' answers can be compared, statistics can be calculated and conclusions can be drawn. Open questions yield **qualitative data**, as participants can give opinions, and the quality of the answer (what is being said) is important. Therefore, data are richer and in more depth. However, qualitative data are harder to analyse because the answers to open questions are potentially all different, so it is difficult to draw general conclusions.

A structured interview is like a questionnaire, in that a set series of questions is used. However, in this case, an interviewer asks the questions and writes down or tapes the answers. There might also be more explanation of the issues. However, unlike a wholly unstructured interview, certain questions do require answers, so that comparisons can be made.

Adorno et al. (1950) used the questionnaire method to find out about the authoritarian personality and its link to prejudice.

Evaluation

+ Questionnaires can be easily distributed, for example by post or around a whole institution. Large quantities can be sent out for completion.
+ The data gathered are largely quantitative, and can be analysed easily. They can also be analysed by computer. This means that, if sampling is good and the response rate is acceptable, firm conclusions, including percentages and comparisons, can be drawn. Conclusions can then be generalised to the target population.
− The response rate is often low. Large numbers of questionnaires can be easily distributed but this may mean that the participant can choose whether or not to complete the questionnaire. If the researcher hands out and collects question-naires personally, the response rate is likely to be higher. Ease of distribution is then no longer an advantage.
− Closed questions (forced-choice ones) restrict possible answers (e.g. *yes*, *no* or *don't know*) and some interesting information can be missed.
− There might be clues in the questions giving the participant an idea of which answer is wanted. These demand characteristics can cause bias, as participants may strive to please the researcher.
− Respondents may give the socially desirable answer, rather than the 'truth'. For example, if asked questions about sensitive issues, such as race, participants would know the socially acceptable answer. They may give that answer rather than what they really think. This is another source of bias.

Note that demand characteristics and social desirability can be sources of bias in other methods too.

Summary

Two research methods used in the social approach

Field experiments

- Done in the participants' natural environment
- Many controls, like laboratory experiments

Advantages
- Good controls, so cause-and-effect relationships suggested
- Natural setting, so fairly valid
- Replicable, so reliable

Disadvantages
- Cannot be controlled as easily as in a laboratory
- Not entirely natural

Surveys

- Questionnaires and structured interviews
- Use closed and open questions, so gather quantitative and qualitative data

Advantages
- Fairly easy to distribute and analyse

Disadvantages
- Poor response rate
- Social desirability and demand characteristics

In-depth areas of study

Obedience

Obedience is when a person obeys instructions from someone else. When someone is in an agentic state, they are acting as an agent for somebody who is telling them what to do. They are showing obedience.

Milgram's obedience study (1963)

Milgram's study is one of the best-known in psychology, and you probably recall it well. It is outlined on pages 37–39. Read it now to recall the main points. You also need to be able to evaluate the study. Then return to this page and read on.

Hofling et al. (1966)

Aim

Hofling et al. carried out a study in a naturalistic setting to look at whether nurses would obey doctors' orders, even when by doing so they would break a number of important rules. To what extent would they obey authority?

Method

A field experiment was set up. Conditions were carefully controlled, and the setting was a hospital, so the surroundings were natural from the nurses' viewpoint.

Procedure

First, when researchers asked them, nurses said they would not obey an instruction that was against the rules. These included the rule that nurses were not supposed to administer a drug without a doctor's signature. Therefore, they were not supposed to act on telephone orders. They were also supposed to check that the doctor giving instructions was a real doctor, and they were supposed to check the dosage.

In the study, an unknown 'doctor' phoned each nurse (there were 22 in the study) and told them to give a patient a dosage of a drug, Astrofen. The dosage was twice the permitted amount (20 mg), and the maximum dosage (10 mg) was written on the packaging. The doctor asked the nurses to administer the drug straightaway and said that he would go to sign the form about 10 minutes later. Three rules were broken: the nurse should have checked the authenticity of the doctor, should not have given the drug without the signature, and should have checked the dosage.

Results
Of the 22 nurses in the study, 21 administered the capsules (which, unbeknown to them, did not contain the drug) to the patient and, therefore, intended to break the rules. Eleven of the nurses said that they had not noticed that there was a problem with the dosage.

Conclusion
This result backed Milgram's claim that we obey instructions even when we don't think we will, and even when we know we should not. The doctor's authority over the nurse was considered to be an important factor — nurses are trained to obey authority figures.

Evaluation

+ This was a field study, so the natural setting meant greater validity. The real nurses thought they received orders from a real doctor, so when they obeyed, to a great extent this was considered to be 'real' obedience. In other words, it was measuring what it claimed to measure — obedience.
+ The procedure is clear and replicable. (It is now hard to replicate, however, because of ethical issues.)
± Hofling et al.'s findings reinforce those of Milgram, although one important difference is that in Milgram's study the participants had to harm another person, whereas in Hofling et al.'s study, the nurses thought they were helping. This suggests that we obey what we perceive as authority, regardless of whether following orders might harm or help others.
− Rank and Jacobson (1977) did not get similar results when they replicated Hofling et al.'s study, which suggests that there might not be reliability.
− The study can be criticised on ethical grounds. The nurses were not given the right to withdraw, and did not give consent. They were debriefed but might have been upset when they realised they had broken the rules in this way.

Two reasons for obedience
Agency theory
Milgram used the idea of an agentic state to explain obedience. The person obeying is in the agentic state — being an agent of the one giving orders. Therefore, the person

giving the orders has the power and is in a position of authority. Once this power relationship is established, the agent will obey orders, and the power of decision-making will be with the one giving the orders. The agent is thus no longer acting under his/her own free will to make decisions, such as when to stop 'giving' electric shocks. The agent obeys because he/she handed power over his/her actions to the one giving the orders. Once in this agentic state, we might potentially do things we would not otherwise (normally) do.

Evaluation

+ Evidence for this explanation of obedience comes from Milgram's studies. Participants said they were just doing what they were told.
+ Through evolution, we may have traits that lead us to live in social groups in which a hierarchical system of power works best. It is likely, therefore, that a system of leaders and followers evolved, with some being the 'agents' of others.
+ If the roles of leaders and followers cannot be explained in evolutionary terms, it could be said that we learn these roles through socialisation (from parents and interacting with others). For example, schools have a clear power structure, which pupils understand.
− In evolutionary terms, it might be thought that an autonomous individual (not in the agentic state but acting under his/her own power) would be more likely to survive. This goes against the explanation for the evolution of hierarchical structures.
− Other explanations for the obedience in Milgram's study include considering elements of the procedure. For example, the experimenter wore a lab coat and the study was at Yale University, which is a formal setting. Milgram's manner was calm, for example when he gave verbal prods to encourage the participant to continue. The calm manner and official setting may have led the participants to trust the situation, so obedience in this study was not like obedience in a real-life setting. In fact, trust was appropriate as no real shocks were given. This is an example of how laboratory experiments might be invalid.

Social power

French and Raven (1959) considered different types of power:
- legitimate — given by role, for example a headteacher
- reward — held by those who distribute rewards, for example an employer
- coercive — held by those who can punish in certain situations
- expert — held by those with specialist knowledge, for example a doctor
- referent — held by people who have the personality to win people over

In his experiment, Milgram had a number of these types of power, which can lead to obedience. He seemed to have:
- legitimate power — he was an experimenter
- reward power — he could reward the participants
- coercive power — he seemed to be able to give shocks to others
- expert power — he was seen as a specialist in a university

Evaluation

+ The idea of power leading to obedience fits in well with agency theory. The agent defers to the power of the leader (in this case the experimenter).
+ The idea of us having evolved as social beings with a hierarchical structure allocating power differently seems sensible, and fits in with our experiences through socialisation (e.g. in school and at home).
− How power is allocated may be seen more as a description of the structure than as an explanation. It could be argued that it does not explain why we defer to different types of power, or why we obey. (However, it fits well with the idea of social roles, socialisation and stereotyping, and is still a useful explanation for obedience.)

Summary

Factors affecting obedience

Findings of studies	Reasons for obedience
• Milgram (1963) showed how we might obey someone's instructions, even when it goes against what we really want to do • Hofling et al.'s (1966) findings supported Milgram • Milgram varied his original study and showed how there was still obedience when the setting was less powerful, although in that case obedience was reduced; he also showed reduced obedience in other situations	• Agency theory • Social power

Prejudice

Prejudice is when people hold stereotypes and let those stereotypes affect their attitudes. Although we can be positively prejudiced in favour of people, usually when we talk about prejudice we are talking about negative hostile attitudes towards a particular group. Discrimination is when a prejudiced attitude leads to prejudiced actions.

Realistic conflict theory

Realistic conflict has been offered as an explanation of prejudice. When groups are in conflict, they tend to become prejudiced against one another. There is real conflict, and this causes groups to change. Those inside the group become the 'in-group' and those outside the group (the others) become the 'out-group'. The out-group becomes stereotyped, and thought of as all the same. The in-group then behaves towards the out-group in ways they would not normally behave. Hostility to the out-group and loyalty to the in-group is called ethnocentrism (centring on one's own culture or group).

Studies have been carried out which set one group against another to see if real conflict leads to prejudice; they have also focused on how to reduce that prejudice

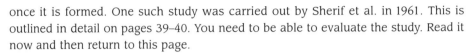

once it is formed. One such study was carried out by Sherif et al. in 1961. This is outlined in detail on pages 39–40. You need to be able to evaluate the study. Read it now and then return to this page.

One criticism of the Sherif et al. study is that the boys were hostile even before the realistic conflict was introduced, so perhaps the formation of groups itself caused the prejudice. This is what social identity theory suggests.

Social identity theory

Tajfel and Turner (1979) put forward the social identity theory — that prejudice is caused by the groups themselves, rather than realistic conflict. The main method used when studying social identity theory (SIT) is to create minimal groups. This means that groups are created casually, with no obvious purpose. One way was to ask participants to pick which of two painters they preferred, Klee or Kandinsky. The paintings of these two artists are similar in style, and participants did not know which painter they had in fact chosen.

The participants were then split randomly into two groups, not taking into account the choice of painter at all. However, participants were told that the two groups were according to the painters chosen. Half were told they had chosen Klee and half were told they had chosen Kandinsky. An important point is that it was not true that the groups were chosen according to their choice of painter. The choice was random, so the groups were formed randomly.

The next step was to find out how the group members behaved towards members of the other group, compared with how they acted with members of their own group. A typical task was to ask how much someone should be paid for an experiment. Participants generally suggested a higher fee for members of their own group (the in-group) than for the others (the out-group). They could tell who was in their group by the numbers allocated to the participants.

Tajfel (1981) suggested that this showed that prejudice comes from simple in-group and out-group separation, even when there is no reason for this, and even when no realistic conflict is present. One explanation for this in-group loyalty, according to social identity theory, is that showing preference to a member of our own group (the in-group) enhances our own status. If we think of our group as worthwhile, our self-esteem is raised.

Evaluation

+ Evidence supports the theory. Crocker and Luhtanen (1990) found that those who show loyalty to the in-group and think highly of it have high self-esteem — this supports social identity theory.

+ Lalonde (1992) gave a different explanation when looking at a poorly performing hockey team. Members of this group could not think they were part of a good team, yet they still showed loyalty to their group. It seemed that this team saw the other team (the out-group) as 'dirtier players', so they felt morally superior; this perhaps explained their loyalty, and raised their self-esteem.

+ Teams studied may be artificial, as were the two groups supposedly formed by painting preference. However, the situation is reasonably realistic, so the study can be considered valid.
+ Minimal group studies have been done in other cultures, with similar outcomes, so the findings seem to be reliable.
- Group members might be competing for status, so this could be a form of realistic conflict. This would then back claims of those who suggest that prejudice is caused by realistic conflict.
- The tasks and settings of many of the studies were unnatural, so there may be bias in the results.

Summary

Two explanations of prejudice	
Realistic conflict theory Sherif et al. (1961) • Simple contact between two groups does not create prejudice • Having to compete against one another does • This competition is realistic conflict	**Social identity theory** Tajfel and Turner (1979) • Prejudice comes from identification with the in-group, which produces hostility to the out-group • Identifying with the in-group raises self-esteem • By raising the status of the in-group, the individual raises his/her own status

Two studies in detail

For this section, you need to know two studies within the social approach, and these are optional. However, for your study of the in-depth areas, you need to know Milgram's (1963) study and Sherif et al.'s (1961) study. These are outlined here. By using these two studies here, the material you have to learn is reduced. However, you can also use any other study you have covered.

Obedience

Milgram (1963)

This is Milgram's main study; variations followed. Some knowledge of these variations would be useful.

Aim

The aim of the study was to test the level of obedience that participants would reach when told to do something as serious as to give another person electric shocks. Milgram was testing whether anyone could have carried out what was inflicted upon the Jews in the Second World War or whether the Germans were different.

Method

A laboratory experiment was carried out at Yale University, testing one participant at a time. Each participant thought that another participant (who was actually a confederate of Milgram's) was getting answers in a test wrong. The severity of electric shocks 'given' by the participant to Milgram's accomplice was observed.

Procedure

Milgram had a confederate who was always 'the learner' in what was supposed to be a memory experiment. The participant was 'the teacher', who was told to give electric shocks of increasing severity as the learner kept 'making mistakes'. The participant thought he or she was the teacher by chance, but the draw to see which role the participant would play was rigged so that he or she was always the teacher.

The learner was in a room where the participant could not see him. The participant sat facing a 'generator' which had levers that indicated shocks from 'small' to 450 volts. Along the generator there were signs such as 'danger' to show that 450 volts was a very high and dangerous voltage to give. The participant was given a slight shock at the start of the study to suggest that the shocks were real. An important part of the study is that, other than this small one, the shocks were not real, and the learner was shouting out in a prepared manner. If the participant showed reluctance, Milgram (who was in the room with the participant) would give verbal prods, such as 'you must go on'.

Milgram wore a grey lab coat and acted calmly throughout. The setting — Yale University — was prestigious and formal.

Results

- 100% of the participants in the main study went up to 300 volts and were prepared to 'shock' another person.
- 65% of the participants went to the highest voltage of 450 volts (26 out of 40 men, and the same number of women).
- Many of the participants showed great distress at having to do this task — even though they continued.

Conclusion

Volunteers were willing to 'shock' another person up to a very high level simply because they got answers wrong in a pretend memory test. This seemed to be solely because they were told to do so by someone in authority.

Evaluation

- + Milgram's study led to a great deal of interest in obedience. Many variations of the study have been conducted, most of which have supported the idea that we do obey orders, often to an unexpected degree.
- + Milgram's study was well controlled, so a cause-and-effect relationship can be claimed.
- + Despite claims to the contrary, Milgram did try to be ethical. He asked colleagues what they thought would happen; no one predicted the high level of obedience,

or the stress caused. He did follow-up interviews with the participants to check that there were no ill effects.

– One criticism is that the procedure was unethical. Right to withdraw was not properly given, and verbal prods were used. Informed consent was not obtained, as the study was said to be about memory. Another instance of deception was that the participants thought the learner was another participant, where he was not. Distress was caused, and many participants were very upset.

– Laboratory experiments, including this one, can be criticised for not being natural. It is perhaps not a valid measure of 'real' obedience. Nevertheless, the participants did obey Milgram's instructions, clearly against their better judgement, as can be seen by their distress and reluctance to continue.

Key Study:

✳ Prejudice

Sherif et al. (1961): the Robber's Cave study

Aim

Sherif et al. (1961) wanted to test the idea that if an in-group and an out-group are created, and conflict is made to develop, prejudice will arise. This is what the realistic conflict theory claims. It was thought that there would be loyalty to the in-group and hostility to the out-group — in other words, ethnocentrism would occur. A further aim was to see whether, after prejudice arose, this prejudice would be reduced if the two groups then had to work together to achieve a common aim.

Method

A field experiment was carried out. The setting (a boys' summer camp) was set up artificially.

Procedure

Twenty White, middle-class boys stayed at the summer camp and were the participants. They were selected as 'normal and ordinary'. They were randomly allocated to one of two groups, which were named 'Rattlers' and 'Eagles'. They did not know about each other at first, but when they did find out about each other, each thought the other group was in their territory. The 'real conflict' part came when Sherif et al. introduced tournaments with team points. This was the first part of the study. After prejudice developed, Sherif et al. set up tasks. First they tried simple contact but this did not reduce prejudice. Then they set tasks involving superordinate goals — for example, the camp water supply had to be restored. These were activities where groups had to work together to succeed in a common goal.

Results

- It was found that real conflict led to prejudice, and the two groups were hostile to one another. Prejudice was measured by, for instance, counting the number of negative words used when referring to the other group.
- When they had to work cooperatively to overcome superordinate goals, prejudice was, to an extent, reduced. Negative words were again counted, and it was clear that there was less name-calling and a better atmosphere.

- In the first stage, when they were hostile to one another, 93% had friends in their own group. However, when working cooperatively, 30% had friends between the groups.

Conclusion

Realistic conflict leads to prejudice, and in-groups become hostile to out-groups if they are in competition. Prejudice to the out-group cannot be reduced by simple contact, but is reduced if the two groups have to work together to achieve a common (superordinate) goal.

Evaluation

+ Field studies such as this have validity, in that they are set up artificially, but the situation is fairly natural.
+ The groups, although randomly formed, were fairly natural, in that boys do form groups in summer camps.
- The boys were all White, middle-class, American, 12-year-olds, so generalising to all groups and all cultures should perhaps be done with care.
- Although fairly natural in terms of setting, the study is in many ways unnatural. The boys were set against one another, and the competitive games were likely to lead to in-group/out-group behaviour. The hostility was predictable, and perhaps not quite the same as prejudice that is experienced in a more 'real' setting.
- The groups seemed to be hostile even before the games began, so the realistic conflict explanation may not be accurate. It may be that any such grouping leads to ethnocentric (in-group/out-group) behaviour.

Summary

Two studies from the social approach

Milgram (1963)	Sherif et al. (1961)
• Participants thought they had given strong shocks to another person • They found this very upsetting • People would obey up to a surprising level	• Realistic conflict caused prejudice • In-groups were hostile to out-groups • Working cooperatively to achieve common goals reduced prejudice

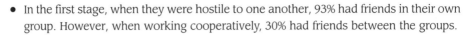

– Key application: reduction of prejudice

Two possible explanations for prejudice are given above: social identity and realistic conflict. There are other explanations too, such as scapegoating. For example, in times of economic hardship, people can become prejudiced against a group, who become scapegoats and blamed for problems unfairly. Such explanations can suggest ways of reducing prejudice. If we look at how prejudice arises, we can try to find ways of reducing it.

Tip

Read the question carefully. An essay asking how prejudice can be *explained* needs different material from an essay asking how prejudice can be *reduced*.

~ Pursuit of common goals (superordinate goals)

Sherif et al.'s (1961) study outlined above (the Robber's Cave study) explains what is meant by superordinate goals, and outlines how aiming for such common goals has the effect of reducing prejudice. The results of the study suggest that the boys became prejudiced when faced with realistic conflict (the tournament and games), and then that prejudice was reduced when the boys had to work together on various tasks, including restoring the camp water supply. You can use the evidence from the study to explain this way of reducing prejudice.

Evaluation

- Sherif et al.'s (1961) study was artificial and was an experiment, so it can be said that we cannot apply the findings to real-life situations and real prejudice.
+ However, it has been shown that divisions between groups can disappear when the groups have to work together for a common goal. For example, in the World Cup, individuals who usually play for different teams, and may therefore be rivals, play together and work as a team to achieve their common goal (or goals!).

~ Equal status contact

Desforges et al. (1991) found that if individuals from different groups come into contact with one another, relationships are improved, especially if these individuals are seen as typical of their group. However, if the experience is bad, this can reinforce negative stereotypes and increase prejudice.

Aronson (1980) suggested that contact between Whites and Blacks in America might be one-sided, in that Blacks are associated with menial jobs. So contact itself might not be enough, as the one-sidedness might increase stereotyping and prejudice.

Deutsch and Collins (1951) studied two housing projects. One project involved segregation while the other had integrated groups. There was less prejudice in the integrated housing project, which suggests that equal status contact reduces prejudice. It is assumed that those within the housing project were of equal status.

Minard (1952) found that miners when underground, and working towards a common goal, had few problems with prejudice. However, after the shift, they did not mix. This suggests that equal status contact at work reduces prejudice, but when people are living separate lives again, prejudice can return.

Evaluation

- These are isolated studies and it is hard to draw general conclusions. For example, in Minard's study, some of the miners may have remained friends above ground. Many groups of workers do not meet outside work, but this does not mean they are prejudiced towards one another.
+ Many of the studies' findings can be explained by considering in-group and out-group behaviour. When working, the miners were an in-group but when not working they would form different groups. Those in the housing projects could

have seen themselves as in-groups; the segregated project thus formed separate in-groups, whereas the integrated project formed one in-group. People of equal status may, for that reason, see themselves as part of the same group, or an in-group. If Blacks work in menial jobs, they are not going to be seen as part of the in-group by those with higher status jobs. In-group and out-group behaviour, as explained by social identity theory, seems to be a good explanation for prejudice, and changing perceptions of the in-group might be a way of reducing prejudice — or redrawing boundaries.

Redrawing boundaries: incorporating in-group with out-group

Turner (1991) pointed out that when the boys in the Sherif et al. (1961) study worked cooperatively, it could be said that they redrew the boundaries between the two groups, and became one in-group. So redrawing the boundary and incorporating others into the in-group can reduce prejudice. Gaertner et al. (1993) did an experiment to test this idea, and found that when two groups became one group to solve a problem, the individuals spoke more positively about each other than when they had been two separate groups. This reinforces the idea that redrawing boundaries to incorporate others into the in-group can reduce prejudice.

Evaluation

+ These findings, showing that incorporating others into the in-group can reduce prejudice, support the claims made about tackling superordinate goals and having equal status. This means that the three suggestions for reducing prejudice outlined above are not contradictory but are presenting similar ideas.

− Redrawing boundaries only reduces prejudice between those now in the in-group; there are bound to be others (the out-group), and prejudice towards them will probably not be reduced. It would be interesting to know if prejudice towards the out-group when the in-group has expanded in this way would be increased.

− Studies like Gaertner's and others in this area are laboratory studies, so they can be criticised as being artificial and not applicable to real-life prejudice.

Summary

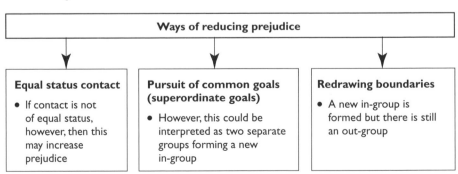

Ways of reducing prejudice		
Equal status contact • If contact is not of equal status, however, then this may increase prejudice	**Pursuit of common goals (superordinate goals)** • However, this could be interpreted as two separate groups forming a new in-group	**Redrawing boundaries** • A new in-group is formed but there is still an out-group

Contemporary issue

In the social approach, you can adapt the key application as a contemporary issue if you wish, and this will mean that you have less material to learn. However, you may have studied a different contemporary issue.

The need to reduce prejudice

Most people would agree that prejudice exists and that it ought to be reduced. Reasons for reducing prejudice can be moral (e.g. we ought not to harm others) or economic (e.g. it can be expensive for society to protect minority groups) or to encourage cooperation between groups. Costs include policing areas and building community relations. Prejudice occurs when people hold stereotypes and let those stereotypes affect their attitudes.

When a prejudiced attitude leads to prejudiced actions, then this is discrimination. The unfairness of prejudice is highlighted by examples such as scapegoating, i.e. when a minority group is blamed for problems it has nothing to do with. In Britain in the 1950s, Black people were encouraged to come to Britain to take up certain jobs that were available. However, prejudice occurred when these people were blamed for unemployment, and it was said that they took the jobs of other people, even though this was not the case.

Reducing prejudice: concepts from the social approach

Sherif et al.'s (1961) study showed that hostility can occur when there is competition. This prejudice was reduced when tasks had to be carried out in cooperation — restoration of the camp water supply, for example. The groups worked together, and then when interviewed the boys had better things to say about those not in their group.

Social identity theory suggests that hostility comes from in-group support: the in-group is hostile to the out-group in order to raise the status of the in-group. So prejudice could be reduced by redrawing boundaries and incorporating others into the in-group.

It could be said that social identity theory explains the reduction of prejudice in the Sherif et al. study, as, when restoring the water supply, the boys worked together, and it could be claimed that a new in-group was formed. It is said that pure contact with others is not enough. In Sherif et al.'s study, the boys were of equal status. It could be that only equal status contact with those of another group will lead to prejudice reduction.

Summary of the social approach

- **Two key assumptions:** the effects of culture and society and the influence of individuals
- **Research methods:** field experiments and surveys
- **In-depth areas of study:** obedience and prejudice

- **Two studies in detail:** for example, Milgram (1963) and Sheriff et al. (1961)
- **Key application:** reduction of prejudice
- **A contemporary issue:** for example, the need to reduce prejudice

The cognitive-developmental approach

Two key assumptions

Key assumptions are underlying beliefs or ideas that underpin an approach.

Cognitive abilities

The cognitive-developmental approach rests on the idea that cognitive abilities develop over time, as a child is growing up. Therefore, an infant does not have the cognitive abilities of a 12-year-old.

Children are not small adults. They see the world in a different way. An example of this is language: infants babble, toddlers use single words, and gradually sentences are formed.

Development in stages

Cognitive development occurs in stages. All children go through the same stages, though not necessarily at exactly the same age. Theorists within this approach differ as to what the stages are, but it is agreed that there is a stepwise progression, where a child's cognitive abilities change, and they can be said to have moved on to the next stage.

Summary

Two key assumptions of the cognitive-developmental approach

The importance of the development of cognitive abilities	Development in stages
• Children are not small adults • They have different cognitive abilities • These abilities develop over time	• Children develop cognitive abilities in stages, although the ages at which these occur are not fixed • An infant does not have the same cognitive abilities as a 12-year-old child

Research methods

Observation

Observations are used in various areas of psychology, including the study of children's development. Rogoff (1981) carried out an observational study in Guatemala, focusing on the whole ecology of the situation, including cultural practices and the social and physical settings. Observations are useful in such situations, as many different factors can be noted and analysed.

Participant observation means the observer is part of the situation and has a role (as well as that of observer). Non-participant observation means the researcher is only watching, and is not part of the situation. Covert observation is done in secret, without the knowledge of the participant(s). Overt observation is done with the knowledge of those being observed. There can be covert participant observation, covert non-partic-ipant observation, overt participant observation, and overt non-participant observation.

Noting everything down can be difficult, so an observer often makes a recording. Categories can be formulated, using a tallying system. The number of instances of a particular action or event within a category can be noted or tallied. Tallying yields quantitative data, whereas recording yields qualitative data.

Evaluation

+ Lots of data, including qualitative data, can be noted. There is a richness and depth that is not often found in experiments, because of the qualitative nature of much of the data gathered.
+ Often a hypothesis is not formulated, and the aim of the study is the main focus, rather than a particular hypothesis. This means that many different facets of a situation can be explored.
+ From the rich, in-depth and varied data that can be gathered by observational methods, hypotheses can be generated and tested. Observations are a good way of exploring new situations.
− One observer might be biased and subjective in his/her recording of data. Inter-observer reliability can be achieved by having more than one observer. However, research is often characterised by having only one observer. Therefore, care must be taken to be as objective as possible.
− The observer(s) might miss important actions or events when they are focusing on something different. It is very hard to capture everything. Thus, the observer is likely to focus on one thing only, which is another possible source of bias.

Longitudinal studies

Longitudinal studies follow one person or a small group over a period of time to record data according to an aim or hypothesis. Experiments can be longitudinal, as can obser-vations and case studies (and indeed other methods), so this is not a method so much as a way of carrying out research using other methods.

Longitudinal studies follow individuals or groups over time, whereas cross-sectional studies investigate individuals or groups at one moment in time. For example, when comparing the language abilities of children at 6 months with children at 3 years, there are two options: a cross-sectional study or a longitudinal study. For a cross-sectional study, the researcher would look at some 6-month-old babies and compare them with some 3-year-old children. A longitudinal study would entail looking at one or more 6-month-old babies and then revisiting the same children when they were 3-year-olds.

An example of a longitudinal study within the cognitive-developmental approach is that of Curtiss (1977) who studied Genie. Genie (not her real name) was a badly neglected child who was found at the age of 13 and whose development had been very poor up to that point. Researchers, including Curtiss, studied Genie in depth for quite a long period to see how the attention they gave her would affect her development. This was therefore a longitudinal case study.

Evaluation

+ The same person or people are studied, so individual differences are controlled.
+ Conclusions are stronger because factors like background and ability are the same throughout the study.
– A problem is that the individual or individuals can drop out, spoiling the whole study. Participants can drop out because they move area, or because they or their parents refuse to continue to be part of the study. Often, more than one person is studied, so the study can continue. However, the effect of people dropping out is still important. The study of Genie was stopped, and so findings were limited to the period of the study.
– The researchers themselves can move area or drop out. This would also stop the study. Similarly, funding might be withdrawn, as happened in the study of Genie.
– Participants might learn what is required in the study through demand characteristics. Over time, the aim of the study might become clear to them, and the findings may reflect this knowledge, which means findings may be biased.

Summary

Two research methods used in the cognitive-developmental approach

Observations	**Longitudinal methods**
• Participant or non-participant • Covert or overt	• Follow one person or a small group over a period of time
Advantage • Can cover lots of different areas	Advantage • Same person/people are studied, so individual differences are controlled
Disadvantage • Can be biased	Disadvantage • Some or all may drop out, and so might the researchers

In-depth areas of study: Piaget and one other

For the in-depth area of study, you need to study Piaget's ideas about children's reasoning, including schemas and operations, as well as his stages. In addition, you need to study one other theorist of your choice.

➤ Jean Piaget

Piaget developed the idea of four stages of development that a child passes through by means of changing schemas and developing cognitive abilities.

Schemas: assimilation, accommodation, adaptation and equilibration

Cognitive abilities develop by means of schemas and change according to experience. A schema is a mental model of what happens in certain situations. For example, a baby develops a schema for sucking by sucking and finding out what happens.

Assimilation occurs as the individual gathers information about what happens under certain circumstances, and the schema is developed in this way (but not yet amended or changed). The information is changed to fit the schema.

Accommodation occurs as new information about what happens means that the existing schema is no longer sufficient for the information, so the schema is changed.

Adaptation is the word for this process of assimilation (adding new information to an existing schema) and accommodation (changing the schema). New schema are developed through the process of adaptation, which means assimilating new information into an existing schema and then accommodating more new information by changing the existing schema.

Equilibration refers to the balance achieved when adaptation has taken place. In equilibration, the individual's schemas suit all the information available, and there is balance. However, the balance does not last long because there are always new experiences, and assimilation and accommodation continue.

Stages according to Piaget

The **sensorimotor stage** is the first stage (0–2 years). Six sub-stages are involved, and babies develop schemas through their senses and their motor movements. Sub-stage 2 involves primary circular reactions, where repeated actions happen just for the pleasure of doing them, such as blowing saliva bubbles (age around 1–4 months). Sub-stage 4 involves developing object permanence, where a baby discovers that an object can go out of sight, such as under a blanket, and still reappear (age around 8–12 months). Adaptation is occurring throughout the stage, and schemas are developing.

The **pre-operational stage** is the second stage (2–6 years). The child in this stage cannot do mental operations, which begin to occur around the age of 7 years, so is 'pre-operational'. Pre-operational children are egocentric, which means they cannot take a viewpoint other than their own. Piaget and Inhelder's (1956) 'mountain' study is outlined below and explains this further. The pre-operational child cannot 'conserve' volume or number. 'Conserving volume' means that a child understands that when a certain volume of liquid is poured from one container to another, even if the containers are different sizes and the level of the liquid is different, there is the same amount of liquid in the new container. 'Conserving number' means that a child understands that even if a row of counters is squashed together to form a shorter row, the number of counters stays the same. Children over the age of 7 can conserve, but pre-operational children cannot.

The **concrete operational stage** is the third stage (6–12 years). At this stage, a child can do 'operations' but needs things or objects to think about. Things and objects are 'concrete' (i.e. real) and can be either present or thought about. Mental operations and activities, such as combining and separating ideas and applying logic, begin to take place. Note that in this stage, the child needs real objects to manipulate when applying logic. They cannot 'operate' mentally without imagining real objects. For example, they can add two cars and four lorries but cannot do abstract mental arithmetic. In this stage, children can decentre and focus on more than one category at a time. For example, if given a set of brown and white wooden beads, they can sort brown and white, but they also understand that there is a category of 'wooden'. The child can see things from another's viewpoint; he or she is no longer egocentric. The child can conserve volume (e.g. knowing that a quantity stays the same even in a different sized container), and so on.

The **formal operations stage** is the fourth stage (12–19 years). The main difference is that the older child can do mental operations using abstract thinking and does not have to manipulate objects either mentally or physically, as they do in the concrete operational stage.

Evaluation

+ The emphasis on discovery learning has led to changes in educational settings, and the emphasis on how children have different cognitive abilities from adults has also helped in making decisions in education. A strength of the theory is that it has useful applications for society.
− Piaget took a lot of data from his own children, so his sample (and he himself) could be said to be biased, although his experiments have been replicated widely.
− It has been argued that development is not stage-like but continuous, and that children learn and develop as they grow.
− Cross-cultural research has, in general, supported the idea of the stages, although it has been said that other cultures do not reach the stage of formal operational thought (e.g. Dasen, 1977). In addition, it has been found that in other cultures, the stages are reached later (e.g. Greenheld, 1966). However, the tasks used to test stages in cognitive development have been said to favour 'Western' culture, so perhaps the children from other cultures were simply not used to the tasks (Hutchins, 1983 and the study of the Caroline Islanders).

Bruner

Jerome Bruner suggested that children's cognitive development progresses through three modes of representation: enactive, iconic and symbolic.

The enactive mode

A baby represents its world by means of actions and not thoughts. The baby learns by experience through actions. Bruner, like Piaget, sees the development of object permanence as important for the developing baby.

The iconic mode

A young child's thinking also develops by means of images or pictures. The child builds a representation of the world consisting of images generalised from experience. They can include past events as well as current ones. This is similar to Piaget's idea that children build schemas, which can be thought of as mental images.

The symbolic mode

Bruner believes that, at around the age of 6, there is a big change in the development of cognition. Through language, a child can move beyond thinking only in images, and can start to think using language — words become symbols for things.

Bruner and Kenney (1966) used an experiment to show the difference between a child using an iconic mode of representation (a way of representing the world in the mind) and a child using a symbolic mode of representation. Bruner's claim is that children can reproduce a display (picture it and rebuild it) at a young age. However, it is only when they are older that they can transpose the display (that is, reproduce it in a different format). To transpose the display, the child uses symbolic thinking. This study is outlined on pages 51–52), so read it now and then return to this page.

Evaluation

+ Bruner's theory is useful in education, where his ideas about using scaffolding have been incorporated. Bruner suggested that children learn better if there is support where it is needed and while it is needed, but that children should also be active learners where possible — doing things for themselves. The emphasis on language is useful, as it shows how explanations can help children to learn.
+ Bruner has also suggested a spiral curriculum, which again emphasises gradual learning. Children are both supported by adults and encouraged to be active explorers.
- Bruner's theory, like those of other cognitive-developmental theorists, can be criticised for focusing too much on stages, whereas development can be seen as continuous.
- It could be claimed that language is used earlier than Bruner suggests, so perhaps the modes are not that separate.

Look up Vygotsky. P.83

Summary

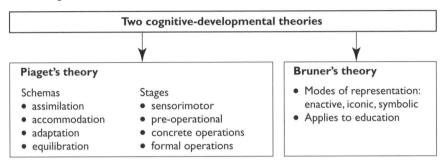

Two cognitive-developmental theories	
Piaget's theory	**Bruner's theory**

Piaget's theory

Schemas
- assimilation
- accommodation
- adaptation
- equilibration

Stages
- sensorimotor
- pre-operational
- concrete operations
- formal operations

Bruner's theory
- Modes of representation: enactive, iconic, symbolic
- Applies to education

Two studies in detail

Egocentrism

Piaget and Inhelder (1956): the mountain task

Aim

This study tested children on their ability to see things from another viewpoint. It was testing egocentrism — a child's inability to look at the world from someone else's view. Children in the pre-operational stage are supposed to be egocentric, but those in the concrete operational stage are not, so children from these two age groups were used.

Method

This was an experiment using a cross-sectional design. It was an independent groups design, as children of different ages are used, and there were two separate groups. The independent variable (IV) was the age of the child and the dependent variable (DV) was whether the child could choose another's viewpoint or not.

Procedure

A mountain scene was created. There were three mountains of different heights, each with a distinguishing feature. One had a church, one had snow and one had a house on top. A doll was positioned on the model. Photographs of various viewpoints were taken, including a picture of what the doll could 'see'. A child participant was asked to walk around the model so that they had seen all sides of it. The child was then seated on one side of the model and a doll positioned on the other side, so that the doll's 'view' was different. The child was asked to pick out the picture the doll could see.

Results

Children in the pre-operational stage tended to pick out the viewpoint they themselves could see, not the viewpoint of the doll.

Conclusion

It was claimed that children in the pre-operational stage were egocentric, and unable to take a different viewpoint. Children in the concrete operational stage could pick out the photo that showed what the doll could see.

Evaluation

+ This experiment is replicable, and has been repeated with the same findings, so it has reliability.

+ The careful sampling and replication, together with good controls, mean the results can be said to be generalisable.

− Other studies have shown that pre-operational children can decentre. Donaldson (1978) explains how a similar study was done using Lego bricks to build walls and then suggesting to a child that a doll had to be hidden from two policeman dolls. The child had to assume that the walls were able to hide the doll and be able to understand what the two policemen could see. Children were able to take the viewpoint of the policeman dolls to say whether or not the doll could be seen. They were not egocentric. Donaldson thought that this was because this task had meaning for the child.

− A weakness, then, is that Piaget and Inhelder's task may not have had meaning for the child. The task perhaps lacked validity, as the Lego task suggests.

− Ethics need to be considered when children are used, although a study such as this is not likely to cause children harm, because it can be treated as a game.

Modes of representation

Bruner and Kenney (1966): the transposition task

Aim

The aim of this study was to test the idea that younger children use an iconic mode of representation, whereas older children use a symbolic mode of representation. It was designed to see if the iconic mode does come before the symbolic mode.

Method

This was an experiment using an independent groups, cross-sectional design. A longitudinal study using a repeated measures design would be possible, but would take longer. The IV was the age of the children; the DV was whether they could reproduce a display having transposed it, or whether they could only reproduce it as they saw it.

Procedure

The display was created by taking a board with nine squares, like a chessboard. Nine pieces of plasticine, progressively wider and taller, were placed as shown below, working from the bottom left square.

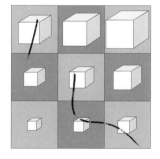

The children were asked to do two tasks. One task was simply to look at the display and reproduce it exactly. The second task was to look at the display and reproduce it, but in a different order, starting with the shortest, thinnest piece on the bottom-right square. This was the transposition task. The reproduction task involved the iconic mode, as the children could visualise the display. The transposition task involved the symbolic mode, as the children had to reason how to transpose the display.

Results

In general, the children could reproduce the display before they could transpose it. 79% of 7-year-olds could do the transposition task but none of the 5-year-olds could. 60% of the 5-year-olds and 80% of the 7-year-olds could do the reproduction task.

Conclusion

This suggests that transposition was a harder task, and that the iconic mode comes before the symbolic mode, which is what Bruner suggested.

Evaluation

+ The study is easily replicated and it seems to be the case that the transposition task is harder. This supports the hypothesis. The study has reliability, as it has been replicated.

+ Bruner went on to suggest ideas for helping children to learn, such as scaffolding. His emphasis on language made his theory different from Piaget's and led to a suggestion that a child's cognitive development could be speeded up by teaching, which has a practical application.

− The task is quite difficult and the children may not have understood what they were required to do. The study lacks validity — as do many such experiments.

Summary

Two studies from the cognitive-developmental approach

Piaget and Inhelder (1956)	Bruner and Kenney (1966)
• The mountain task • Children are egocentric in the pre-operational stage	• 5-year-olds can do a reproduction task • 7-year-olds can do a transposition task • Iconic mode comes before symbolic mode

Key application: influences on education

The key application for the cognitive-developmental approach is its use in education. This has already been mentioned in the evaluation of Piaget's and Bruner's theories. Two main ways in which the theories have been applied to education are outlined here. There are others, and an idea from Vygotsky (another cognitive-developmental theorist you may have studied) is also outlined below.

Discovery learning

Piaget's views of how children move through the four stages of cognitive development suggest that children have to learn for themselves, and have to build schemas through assimilation and accommodation. These are active processes — the children must have the experiences for themselves. So in education, from nursery onwards, children need to have stimulation and materials to enable discovery and building of schemas.

- Young children will not follow logical arguments.
- Tasks must be interesting so that children will explore.
- Children must be pushed into disequilibrium so that they have to accommodate and build new schemas.
- The learning process is more important than the facts.
- Social experiences can help to build schemas, so small groups are useful.
- A curriculum must fit the child; children are at different stages (they are individuals).

The spiral curriculum

Bruner thought that increasing the level of difficulty for children was a successful way of getting them to move from the iconic mode of representation to a symbolic mode of thought. Rather than learning facts one after another, children should learn skills and principles, so that they can find out facts for themselves.

Bruner's ideas are similar to those of Vygotsky. The zone of proximal development put forward by Vygotsky suggests that children should go beyond what they can do, and should extend into something they cannot quite reach. For example, children should not just read what they are able to read but should try reading for meaning even when they cannot manage all the words — so they are pushing at the boundaries of what they can manage. This helps them to learn, and is similar to Bruner's idea of a spiral curriculum.

Collaborative learning

Vygotsky suggests that children should not be taught facts (Piaget and Bruner agree on this). Teachers can help children to learn by pushing them to do things they cannot really manage, within the zone of proximal development. However, members of a child's peergroup can also help — a process of collaborative learning. Children who can do something can help those who cannot, and they learn from each other. The children doing the 'teaching' learn by having to express themselves, and the ones being taught also learn. Cooperation, rather than competition, is important.

> **Evaluation**
>
> ± Research has tended to take place in primary schools, although collaborative learning seems to help with older children too. It is hard, however, to generalise beyond the research carried out, and the ideas outlined above refer to primary school aged children.

± There are many similarities in the suggestions of Piaget, Bruner and Vygotsky, and their ideas have been successfully implemented in schools. The main difference is that Piaget's ideas suggest that a child learns at his/her own pace, which cannot be speeded up, whereas the other two have ideas for helping a child to learn more quickly and more successfully.

± If considering the idea of student-centred learning versus the idea of didactic teaching (where a teacher presents facts), then the above ideas can be used in favour of student-centred learning. However, remember that the ideas apply mainly to children of primary school age.

Summary

Applying cognitive-developmental theories to education		
Piaget — discovery learning	**Bruner — spiral curriculum**	**Vygotsky — collaborative learning**
• Children build schemas through experiences • Early education must provide these experiences and the right materials	• Children can be taught to move to the symbolic mode • They need to learn principles, not facts • They can discover the facts for themselves	• Children can help each other • Peer teaching is successful • Group work is useful

Contemporary issue

In the cognitive-developmental approach, you can adapt the key application as a contemporary issue if you wish, and this means that you will have less material to learn. (However, you may have studied a different contemporary issue.) Here, the issue is collaborative versus whole-class teaching, which links to the key application for this approach.

Whole-class teaching or group learning?

Here is a brief extract from an article in the *Times Educational Supplement*, 29 September 2000, p. 26.

It is claimed that junior school pupils spend two-thirds of their classroom time working individually. Why do such children spend most of their time sitting in groups if so much of their work is done individually? Group seating is ideal for collaborative work, but a classroom set out in rows or pairs of tables would suit individual work better, and pupils would concentrate more. Children sitting in rows or pairs spend between 16% and 124%

more of their time 'on task' (focusing on what is to be done) than when seated in groups. Children who are easily distracted spend 80% more time on task when sitting in rows.

The evidence in this article dates back 20 years, and it is suggested elsewhere in the article that setting a room out in rows is now frowned upon. It is suggested that it is not always feasible to move a room around within a day's teaching; that inspectors do not approve of a room set out in rows; and that teachers do not learn enough about different classroom layouts while training. However, where rooms are reorganised during the day, it is thought that fewer children would be 'struggling to work in contexts that do not support their learning'. In the article, a teacher's room layout is outlined, and it is mentioned that she takes care to leave a set of tables positioned to one side as a focus group table. This is used continually for intensive teacher–pupil group work.

Applying concepts from the cognitive-developmental approach

Collaborative learning, as supported by the work of Vygotsky, is mentioned in the article as being a useful technique which requires tables set out in groups. However, it is claimed that junior pupils spend only 30% of their time on such group work. This suggests that, at least at junior school age, children are not using discovery learning methods or collaborative learning all the time. The existence of a focus group table, which is used continually, suggests that something like scaffolding is taking place. The intensive teacher–pupil group work is seen as essential, and suggests that simple discovery learning without one-to-one support is not advocated; neither is rote learning. The mention of tables set out in groups is evidence of the work of cognitive-developmental theorists being taken into account. Collaborative learning is still in evidence — even though this article suggests that in some work, concentration is improved if children work alone.

look up "Do computers help people learn" P.93

Summary of the cognitive-developmental approach

- **Two key assumptions:** 'the importance of cognition' and 'development in stages'
- **Research methods:** observations and longitudinal studies
- **In-depth areas of study:** Piaget's theories and, for example, those of Bruner
- **Two studies in detail:** for example, Piaget and Inhelder's (1956) mountain task and Bruner and Kenney's (1966) transposition task
- **Key application:** applying cognitive-developmental concepts to education (for example, discovery learning, the spiral curriculum and collaborative learning)
- **A contemporary issue:** for example, the whole-class teaching versus group learning debate

Questions
&
Answers

The questions that follow are presented in three sections, one for each of the approaches.

Choose one approach and revise the material using this unit guide. Work through the questions for your chosen approach, answering them yourself without reading the advice on how to answer the question and without reading the answer given. Then mark your own answers, and read through the advice on what is required. Did you interpret the question successfully? Read through the answers given and note where the marks are awarded. Finally, read through the examiner's comments to see what a full answer should include.

Once you have prepared answers for all the questions in a particular approach, answer them again but this time choose a different topic. For example, if you answered a question on a key assumption, then answer it again using the other assumption that you have prepared. If you have described a study within the approach, then describe your other chosen study. If the question is about one in-depth area (e.g. memory), then answer it as if it were about the other in-depth area (e.g. forgetting).

Examiner's comments
All questions and answers are followed by examiner's comments. These are preceded by the icon ✏. They indicate where credit is due and point out areas for improvement, specific problems and common errors such as poor time management, lack of clarity, weak or non-existent development, irrelevance, misinterpretation of the question and mistaken meanings of terms.

Section 1

The cognitive approach

Key assumptions

(1) Outline *one* key assumption of the cognitive approach. (3 marks, AO1)

(2) Give *two* key assumptions of the cognitive approach. (2 marks, AO1)

(3) In the boxes below, tick the *two* statements that apply to the cognitive approach. (2 marks, AO1)

We are guided strongly by our unconscious	☐
There are similarities in the ways computers and brains operate	☐
Information is processed by the brain; there is input, processing and output	☐
Children develop through set stages	☐

e **(1)** Say three things about a key assumption of this approach. 1 mark is likely to be for knowing the assumption (naming it), and 2 further marks for saying more about it. An example is a useful idea, but keep it short as it will not be worth 2 marks.

(2) Here, just stating two key assumptions is fine. You do not have to say more about them.

(3) Two ticks are required — no crosses. Just put a tick against each of two statements that you think are correct.

Answers to key assumptions questions

(1) The mind/brain processes information like a computer. ✓ We take information in, and then it is subjected to mental processes. ✓ There is input, processing and then output. ✓

e This is a clear and concise answer. 1 mark is given for the assumption, in this case the computer analogy. 1 mark is awarded for linking this to the processing of information and 1 mark for expanding on this by mentioning input, processing and output. An example, such as the Atkinson and Shiffrin (1968) model, could also be offered for a possible mark.

(2) Information processing — that we process information in a linear fashion. ✓ Computer analogy — that our brains work like computers. ✓

e This is all that is required, as the question does not ask for outlines or descriptions. The full 2 marks are awarded.

(3)

We are guided strongly by our unconscious	☐
There are similarities in the ways computers and brains operate	☑ ✓
Information is processed by the brain; there is input, processing and output	☑ ✓
Children develop through set stages	☐

e These choices are correct, for 2 marks.

Common research methods

**(4) Give *one* strength and *one* weakness of the experiment as a research
method.** (4 marks, AO2)

**(5) Describe how the case-study method has been used in the cognitive
approach.** (4 marks, AO1)

> *e* **(4)** There are 2 marks for the strength and 2 marks for the weakness. Don't just
> give an answer for each: be sure to expand it enough for the full 2 marks. For
> example, say what the strength is, and then expand on what you mean.
>
> **(5)** You can get some marks for giving an example of the use of a case study in this
> approach. However, you also need to say how case studies are used — for
> example, what they are used for. Alternatively, you could explain directly how
> they are used, by spelling out the procedure.

Answers to common research methods questions

(4) A strength is that it is well controlled. A weakness is that you cannot see natural
behaviour, as the experiment is in a laboratory. ✓

> *e* The weakness gets 1 mark because the answer clearly and effectively communi-
> cates that natural behaviour is not found in a laboratory. For the additional mark,
> this needs elaborating, perhaps mentioning the lack of validity, or saying that the
> unnatural situation means that what is being measured is not 'normal'. The strength
> does not earn a mark. The answer needs to say *what* is well controlled, and how
> that means that a study can be repeated to see if the same results are found, which
> means it has reliability.

(5) Brain-damaged people have been observed with regard to their STM and LTM. ✓
Many have been found to have little or no LTM but to be able to learn new tasks.
Evidence like this is used to support models like the multi-store model. ✓ By
looking at what damage is done, and what effect this has on memory, we can see
which part of the brain does what. ✓ HM and KF were both case studies. ✓

> *e* This answer gets all 4 marks. The examples are useful, and there is an introduc-
> tory statement saying how case studies are used (briefly mentioning observation).
> The candidate shows that these are used as evidence for theories, and finally
> demonstrates how they are used to link cognitive abilities (or lack of them) to
> damaged areas of the brain.

■ ■ ■

In-depth area(s) of study

(6) Outline *one* theory of forgetting. (3 marks, AO1)

**(7) Evaluate *one* theory or model of memory in terms of *two* of the following
criteria: methodological issues, ethical issues, alternative theories, research
evidence for contradictory claims, or its practical application.** (6 marks, AO2)

(8) For *one* model/theory of memory that you have studied, complete the following table.

(3 marks, AO1)

Name of the model/theory (1 mark)	
One aspect of the model/theory (1 mark)	
One problem with the model/theory (1 mark)	

e **(6)** Giving one theory of forgetting earns you the first mark. Then there are 2 more marks for expanding on your answer. Say what the theory is, and make sure you say enough about it for the 2 extra marks.

(7) You have to do two things here, and there are 6 marks, so there are 3 marks for each task. Choose one of the criteria (e.g. ethical issues) and say three things about ethical issues in relation to your chosen theory of memory. Then choose one of the other criteria (e.g. alternative theories) and say three things about alternative theories.

(8) There is 1 mark for each element. You do not need to say much for 1 mark. The first mark is for naming the model (or identifying it if you cannot recall the name of the theory or the name(s) of the researchers). The second mark is for saying something about that model — for example, if looking at the Atkinson and Shriffin model, saying that the focus is on two stores: STM and LTM. The third mark is for saying something to criticise it.

Answers to in-depth area(s) of study questions

(6) Retrieval failure — the cues for recall ✓ do not match the encoding that takes place in memory. ✓

e Retrieval failure due to lack of cues scores 1 mark for the theory, and the additional information about cues not matching encoding gets another mark. However, this is not a very clear outline of a theory of forgetting. The candidate needed to be clearer, to talk about cue-dependent forgetting, and mention state and context dependency. This answer scores 2 marks out of 3.

(7) The multi-store model has stimulated much research into the mind to identify exactly how memory is used and stored. This stimulated research by Baddeley and Hitch ✓ who came up with the working memory (WM) model. The WM model expands STM to look at four different areas. ✓ These include an articulatory loop,

section

a visuospatial scratchpad and a central executive. ✓ Research is based on experimental evidence, which is said to lack validity, as artificial tasks are used. ✓

✐ The first criterion covered is alternative theory, and for this the full 3 marks are
gained. 1 mark is for the mention of the model having stimulated research such as
the working memory model. The second mark is for mentioning the four areas of
the working model, and the third mark for elaborating on this. The second
criterion is methodological issues, and a mark is given for mentioning the artificial
nature of experiments used. This could have been expanded by means of an
example, or at least explained more fully, for the final 2 marks. For example, it
could be said that learning lists under water is not a normal thing to do.

(8)

Name of the model/theory (1 mark)	Levels of processing — Craik and Lockhart (1972)
One aspect of the model/theory (1 mark)	Three levels of processing are found — structural, phonemic and semantic
One problem with the model/theory (1 mark)	Circular, in not really explaining anything; better recall comes from deeper processing, and we show deeper processing by pointing to better recall

✐ Each of the above answers scores 1 mark. When only 1 mark is available, remember
that you do not have to write a great deal.

■ ■ ■

Two studies

(9) **Describe *one* study from the cognitive approach.**   (5 marks, AO1)

(10) **Evaluate *one* study from the cognitive approach.**   (5 marks, AO2)

(11) **Discuss *one* study from the cognitive approach.**   (10 marks, essay)

✐ **(9)** Note that just describing what was done in the study (the procedure), or what
was found (the results or findings), is not enough for all 5 marks. For the first
mark, make sure the study is identifiable. A further mark can be gained by
saying why the study was done. 2 marks can be gained by saying what was done,
and 2 more marks for what was found (the results). Marks can also be gained
by giving the conclusion. There are more ways than one to get the 5 marks. Be
sure to write enough, as for 5 marks you are trying to say five things.

(10) Evaluation can come in many forms. You can give ethical issues (good and/or
bad), alternative theories or studies, methodological problems (such as the
reliability of experiments or the limitations of case studies), or criticisms of the

study itself. Be sure to write enough for 5 marks. You are trying to say five things, although it is possible to gain more than 1 mark for a good, well made point.

(11) In this essay question, 2 marks are for clarity and communication. These marks are gained by correct use of terms, good spelling, and using continuous prose (i.e. not writing in note form). 2 marks are for balance and breadth. These marks are earned by giving a good balance of AO1 (knowledge and understanding) and AO2 (evaluation and comment). This leaves 3 AO1 marks and 3 AO2 marks. You need to say three clear things about the study, and make three clear points in evaluation. You could answer this using the same material as for (a) and (b) above. Make sure you link the points made, to form a discussion.

Answers to two studies questions

(9) Baddeley wanted to see if context helps recall. ✓ He and a colleague asked divers to learn a list of words under water. ✓ Then half the divers recalled the list above water and the other half recalled the list while diving. ✓ Those who were diving recalled more words. ✓ It was decided that context does aid recall. ✓

> *e* 1 mark is given for knowing the Godden and Baddeley study. Note that you do not have to name the study precisely. Mentioning Baddeley and divers is enough for it to be identifiable. 2 more marks are given for the procedure (memorising the list underwater, then half recalling above water). 1 mark is given for the results (they recalled more when diving) and a further mark is given for a conclusion (context does aid recall).

(10) Using the above study (Baddeley), it is not possible to know how good each diver's memory was in the first place. Some people have better memories than others, so there could have been a bias in the sampling. ✓✓ However, other studies have confirmed the results — that context is important. ✓ Another problem is the unnatural nature of the task, and it could be said that the study is not valid. Divers do not usually learn lists of words under water. ✓✓

> *e* This answer scores full marks. It is difficult to mark sentence by sentence — on two occasions the first mark is given mainly because of the second point. For example, just mentioning the difference in memory of divers may not get a mark on its own. The first mark is given partly because of the second point, that this could lead to bias in the sampling. The point about other studies earns a further mark. The final two points, like the first two points, score a double mark. The unnatural nature of the task is important, but the candidate needs to say why. This answer is elaborated in the final sentence.

(11) Loftus and Palmer (1974) carried out a study to look at the effect of leading questions on recall. They did an experiment using an independent groups design. All participants watched a film that included a car accident. ✓ (AO1) Participants had to answer questions based on the film. One question in particular was varied. Some participants were asked how fast the cars were going when they 'hit', some had the word 'smashed' and there were also other words such as 'bumped' and 'collided'. ✓ (AO1) The researchers found that the estimate of the speed varied according to the 'seriousness' of the verb used. The participants with the word 'hit' gave a slower speed estimate than the participants with the word 'smashed'. Later, the same participants were asked about broken glass at the scene (there was no broken glass). Those with the word 'smashed' were more likely to 'remember' broken glass. ✓ (AO1, max) The conclusions of this and other similar studies were applied to point out that eyewitness testimony could be swayed by leading questions, and this has helped the justice system. ✓ (AO2) However, the experiment was unnatural, taking place in an artificial setting, and the accident was filmed, not real. ✓ (AO2) There was no real emotion involved, which there might be in a real situation, so perhaps the conclusions drawn were not valid. ✓ (AO2, max)

e This is a well constructed essay, giving one clear study as asked. The answer focuses first on describing the study and then on evaluating it. The description could have gained more marks but there are only 3 AO1 marks available. Note the clear evaluation points. There is correct use of terms, while spelling and grammar are good, for full communication and clarity marks. There is a good range of AO1 and AO2 points, for full balance and breadth marks. This essay scores 10 marks.

■ ■ ■

Key application

(12) Discuss what research has shown about eyewitness testimony.   (10 marks, essay)

e In this essay question, 2 marks are for clarity and communication. These marks are gained by correct use of terms, good spelling, and use of continuous prose (i.e. not writing in note form). 2 marks are for balance and breadth, gained by giving a good balance of AO1 (knowledge and understanding) and AO2 (evaluation and comment). This leaves 3 AO1 marks and 3 AO2 marks, so you need to say three clear things about eyewitness testimony and make three evaluative points.

Answer to key application question

(12) There are two memory stores, STM and LTM. If material is rehearsed, it goes from STM into LTM but otherwise it is forgotten. STM holds around seven pieces of information, and LTM can hold as much information as you want. Another memory model shows that it is the depth of processing that makes us remember more. With eyewitness testimony, not much is remembered because of the emotion of the situation. ✓ (AO1)

e Only one point is made that focuses on the question, so only 1 mark is given for content. Although the written material is well presented, there are few appropriate terms, so only 1 clarity and communication mark is given. There is enough balance and breadth for 1 mark, giving a total of 3 marks out of 10.

Contemporary issue

(13) **Outline** *one* **contemporary issue or debate that can be explained using the cognitive approach.** (3 marks, AO1)

(14) **Explain how the cognitive approach can help us to understand this issue or debate.** (6 marks, AO2)

(15) **Use your knowledge of the cognitive approach in psychology to describe and explain** *one* **contemporary issue or debate.** (12 marks, essay)

(13) You need to describe the issue here. Try to avoid applying theories if you can. Some issues are hard to separate from theories, for example the unreliability of eyewitness testimony. However, for this answer you need to give the issue (e.g. the unreliability and the problems for justice). 1 mark is usually for the issue itself and 2 further marks are for saying more about it.

(14) For this part of the question, you need to apply psychology to the issue outlined in your answer to question 13. There are many ways of doing this and any useful contribution — where you link psychological understanding to the issue, using the right approach — gains marks. You need to say quite a lot for 6 marks, and examples can be useful. You could aim to apply two or three concepts for 3 marks, and gain the other marks by saying more about them.

(15) In this essay question, 2 marks are for clarity and communication (correct use of terms, good spelling, and using continuous prose (i.e. not writing in note form). 2 marks are for balance and breadth. This requires a good balance of AO1 (knowledge and understanding) and AO2 (evaluation and comment), as well as describing the issue briefly and applying concepts. This leaves 4 AO1 marks and 4 AO2 marks. 1 mark will be for the issue itself. The other marks are gained using material similar to that in questions 13 and 14 above, but do not spend too long outlining the issue. Spend time outlining the psychology and then be sure to evaluate and comment.

Answers to contemporary issue questions

(13) Eyewitness testimony (EWT), which has been relied on heavily in court, may not be as reliable as was thought. ✓ Convictions are brought about because of the evidence from eyewitnesses, and if it can be shown that there are many factors that bring bias to such evidence, then juries should perhaps be warned that eyewitness evidence may need to be questioned. ✓✓

The issue is the unreliability of EWT, and this gets a mark. 2 more marks are given for the detailed sentence claiming that EWT can be affected by many factors, and that juries might need to be aware of this.

(14) Confabulation occurs when we fit information that we think might be relevant into our memory of an event. ✓ We don't just witness something — we use schemas and previous experiences to interpret what we are seeing. ✓ This can lead to false testimony, even though the witness thinks he/she is telling it as it is. ✓ Loftus has done a lot of research in this area, and has also found that leading questions can bias EWT. ✓ A study showed that when asked the speed when cars 'hit', a lower estimate was given than when asked to estimate the speed when the cars 'smashed'. ✓

> *e* Five good points are made here, for 5 marks, with two main concepts being used from the approach. First, the answer looks at confabulation and schemas, showing how testimony can be biased, for 3 marks. Second, the answer looks at leading questions and the work of Loftus. This earns 2 marks. A further mark is needed, which could be gained from elaboration — perhaps mentioning another study, or the 'broken glass' example.

(15) The usefulness of eyewitness testimony is an issue explained in cognitive psychology. The police rely on eyewitness memory both when finding out who is responsible for a crime and in court when prosecuting. Juries often have to make their decision based on eyewitness testimony. So if it is unreliable, that is an important issue. ✓ (AO1) Loftus did many studies in this area and found out that eyewitness testimony can be unreliable. Leading questions can change memories, and experiments have shown this. ✓ (AO1) For example, if asked about 'a' broken headlight, you are less likely to 'recall' one than if asked about 'the' broken headlight — so the wording of a question can be very important. ✓ (AO1) However, these were laboratory studies, and therefore in an unnatural setting doing unnatural tasks. ✓ (AO2) The emotion of a real incident was missing, so the conclusions may not be valid. ✓ (AO2) A good point is that the studies could be repeated, so could be said to be reliable, and many studies have shown that EWT is unreliable. ✓ (AO2) It was also found that odd bits of information, like whether there was a broken headlight, might be changed by leading questions, but that possibly the most important information was not so changeable. ✓ (AO2)

> *e* This is a good, clear essay. 1 mark is given for the issue, which is outlined well. 1 mark is given for mentioning Loftus's studies and giving an example, and another mark is given for pointing to leading questions. The evaluation (AO2) marks are gained and full marks are given for four good points made. One more AO1 mark is needed and could have been gained with one example other than Loftus (e.g. the Loftus and Palmer (1974) study). The essay covers the material well, so full balance and breadth marks are given, and it is well written, so full clarity and communication marks are also awarded. 11 marks out of 12 are awarded.

The social approach

Key assumptions

(1) Outline *one* key assumption of the social approach. (3 marks, AO1)

(2) Give *two* key assumptions of the social approach. (2 marks, AO1)

(3) In the boxes below, tick the *two* statements that apply to the social approach. (2 marks, AO1)

Individuals cannot be understood outside their culture	☐
Interactions between people are important	☐
Information is processed by the brain; there is input, processing and output	☐
Children develop through set stages	☐

(1) Say three things about a key assumption of this approach. 1 mark is likely to be for knowing the assumption (naming it), and 2 further marks for saying more about it. An example is a useful idea, but keep it short as it will not be worth 2 marks.

(2) Here, just stating two key assumptions is fine. You do not have to say more about them.

(3) Two ticks are required — no crosses. Just put a tick against each of two statements that you think are correct.

Answers to key assumptions questions

(1) The social approach focuses on the unconscious. There are three parts of the personality: the id, the ego and the superego.

Unfortunately, this answer is about the psychodynamic approach, so no marks are awarded.

(2) One assumption of the social approach is that how we interact with others is important in studying our behaviour ✓. Another assumption is that we act as part of a group within a culture, rather than as isolated individuals. ✓

Two assumptions are given briefly, which is all that is asked for, so full marks.

(3)

Individuals cannot be understood outside their culture	☑	✓
Interactions between people are important	☑	✓
Information is processed by the brain; there is input, processing and output	☐	
Children develop through set stages	☐	

The ticks show the correct statements, for 2 marks.

■ ■ ■

Common research methods

(4) Give *one* strength and *one* weakness of surveys as a research method. (4 marks, AO2)

section

(5) Describe *one* **research method that has commonly been used in the social approach.** (4 marks, AO1)

> *(4)* There are 2 marks for the strength and 2 marks for the weakness. Do not just give an answer for each — be sure to expand it enough for the full 2 marks. For example, say what the strength is, and then say something else to explain it further.

> **(5)** Focus on description, not evaluation, here. For example, if you choose to describe the questionnaire method, then be sure to describe *what takes place*. Mention open and closed questions, what type of data are gathered, and so on. For this question, do not say what is good and bad about the method — just say what it is. An example is a good idea, but avoid giving too much detail, as an example does not itself describe the method.

Answers to common research methods questions

(4) One strength is that a lot of people can be reached relatively cheaply by posting surveys or by handing them out in busy areas. Compared with an experiment, there can be many participants. ✓✓ A weakness is that there can be a poor response rate. When a lot of people are asked, it is likely that many will not post the questionnaire back, or that people will refuse to complete it if asked personally. ✓✓

> A strength and a weakness are correctly identified, for 1 mark each, and there is some expansion in each case, so full marks.

(5) Experimental method: A study is set up controlling as many variables as possible. ✓ One variable is changed (the IV) and the outcome is measured (the DV). ✓ This shows that there is a cause-and-effect relationship between the two. ✓

> Experiments are common within the social approach, so this method is fine. Controlling variables is an important part of an experiment, so 1 mark is given here. The important point about manipulation of an IV to measure a DV also gets a mark, as does the reference to finding a cause-and-effect relationship. More needs to be said for the fourth mark, perhaps mentioning different types of design, or the importance of sampling. Briefly mentioning an example, such as Milgram, would also be useful.

■ ■ ■

In-depth area(s) of study

(6) What is meant by the term 'obedience'? (2 marks, AO1)

(7) Outline Milgram's agency theory of obedience. (3 marks, AO1)

(8) Evaluate social identity theory as an explanation of prejudice. (4 marks, AO2)

🖉 **(6)** You need to give a definition of obedience. A simple definition will gain 1 mark and a more detailed definition will gain 2 marks.

(7) There are 3 marks here, all for outlining what is meant by the agency theory. An example is a good idea, but keep it short as it will be worth no more than 1 mark. However, it will help to illustrate your answer and show that you understand the theory.

(8) In a unit test, you probably would have been asked to say what social identity theory is before being asked this question. Note that for 'evaluate' questions you do not have to describe at all. Assume that the examiner knows what the theory is. All 4 marks are for evaluation. You could say what the theory explains, or say if another theory explains prejudice better or contradicts this one, or criticise the methods used to arrive at the theory (perhaps researchers used laboratory experiments that are not valid).

Answers to in-depth areas of study questions

(6) Obedience is when people obey others in authority. ✓

🖉 It is not adding much to say that obedience is when people obey, but saying that they obey people in authority is enough for 1 mark. For full marks, this needs more detail, such as mentioning that obeying means you are in an agentic state, or saying that it differs from conformity in that someone is acting upon orders.

(7) In Milgram's study, the participants denied to themselves that they were responsible for their actions. They allowed the experimenter to take responsibility for what was happening. When you are not acting under your own control but because of the orders of someone else, you are their agent, and this is being in an agentic state. ✓✓

🖉 2 marks are awarded here for saying what an agentic state is. The final mark would be gained by linking this to Milgram's study and showing how the participants said they felt they had to continue, and they were just obeying orders. This was his agency theory of obedience — that people were not making their own decisions.

(8) Many studies have shown that we prefer our in-group and are less interested in any out-group. Tajfel did a lot of work in this area, and others have too. It seems that we boost our self-esteem by siding with an in-group, which means going against an out-group. So social identity theory (SIT) seems a reasonable explanation. ✓ It can also explain other studies of prejudice. For example, Minard's miners study could have shown that the miners were an in-group when working, but when above ground they were no longer an in-group (not being 'miners' any more but going home to different roles). ✓✓ However, much of the research was done using experiments and falsely formed groups, so the conclusions might not be valid. ✓

e Full marks are gained here. 1 mark is awarded for saying that there is a lot of evidence (although this needs elaboration, as is done here). 2 further marks are given for the Minard example and showing how SIT can explain it. The final mark is for the methodological criticism.

■ ■ ■

Two studies

(9) Describe *one* study from the social approach. (5 marks, AO1)
(10) Evaluate *one* study from the social approach. (5 marks, AO2)
(11) Outline the findings of *two* studies from the social approach. (6 marks, AO1)

e **(9)** Note that just describing what was done in the study (the procedure), or what was found (the results or findings), is not enough for all 5 marks. For the first mark, make sure the study is identifiable. A further mark can be gained by saying why the study was done. 2 more marks can be gained by saying what was done, and 2 marks for saying what was found (the results). Marks can also be earned for giving the conclusion. There are more ways than one to get the 5 marks.

(10) Evaluation can come in many forms. You can give ethical issues (good and/or bad), alternative theories or studies, methodological problems (such as the reliability of experiments or the limitations of case studies) or criticisms of the study itself. Be sure to write enough for 5 marks. You are trying to say five things, although it is possible to gain more than 1 mark for a good, well made point.

(11) Two things are being asked here (the findings of two studies), so 3 marks are available for each. Say three things about the results or findings of one study for 3 marks, and the same for the other study. Focus on results; do not describe what happened in the studies, but do make sure they are identifiable.

Answers to two studies questions

(9) Hofling: studied a group of 22 nurses. ✓ The nurses were on duty and were given instructions over the phone by a doctor who wanted them to give a patient a dosage of a drug — this dosage would have been too high. ✓ Although the nurses should not have taken instructions over the phone, and they should have checked the dosage, 21 out of the 22 nurses obeyed the doctor. ✓ They were stopped before the drug was administered, and there was no real medication in any case. ✓

e The first mark is given for identifying a correct study. Then there is 1 mark for the procedure, although a little more detail would have earned 2 marks. The main result (21 out of 22 obeyed) is given, for 1 mark. Finally, a mark is awarded for the information that they were stopped and in any case there was no real drug, as this is elaboration upon the procedure. A further mark could have been gained by drawing a clear conclusion about obedience to authority.

(10) Hofling: The nurses were carrying out instructions following the doctor's authority. As part of the study, a control group was asked if they would obey instructions such as those given in the study, and they all said they would not. This shows that the situation we are in and the social pressure at the time influences our behaviour, which is a useful contribution. ✓✓ As this study was a field study and took place in a real hospital with real nurses, it was thought to be stronger evidence of obedience than Milgram's artificial laboratory study. ✓✓

> *e* 2 marks are scored for pointing out the usefulness of the contribution, and 2 marks for comparing the study with Milgram's and showing that Hofling's study is arguably more valid. The first double mark is given because simply outlining the control group questions, without evaluation or comment, would not gain any marks. The information helps to explain the point that the study found that the pressure of a situation made a difference.

(11) Milgram found that people obey an authority figure even to the point of thinking they might have killed someone ✓. Hofling found that nurses obey a doctor's orders even when obeying them is against the rules. ✓

> *e* There are two studies here, and the findings are stated, for 2 marks, but not enough information is given for 6 marks. Both sentences give nearly enough for another mark. This answer needs to be expanded more clearly; for example, by adding that all the participants went up to 300 V and 65% went up to 450 V, or that 21 of the 22 nurses obeyed orders. This was against the findings of a survey in which nurses said they would not obey such an instruction.

■ ■ ■

Key application

(12) Read the source below. Then explain what is being said, using concepts from the social approach. *(6 marks, AO2)*

> Fighting broke out between two local villages when a visiting rugby team from one of the villages won an annual competition by 28 points. At first, the fight was only between two of the players who had clashed during the match, but soon the fighting spread and police had to be called. Elders from one of the villages explained that there had been prejudice between the two villages for years, ever since a factory was built near one village bringing good road links and jobs, whereas the other village was in another valley, and did not have the same advantages.

(13) Theories from the social approach have helped to explain how prejudice may be formed, but have also shown how it might be reduced. Discuss how prejudice can be reduced. *(12 marks, essay)*

> *e* **(12)** The 6 marks are all for applying ideas from the social approach. Aim for two or three concepts or ideas, and then explain them to get the full marks. If you use two ideas, explain each more fully. Link to the source at least once.

(13) In this essay question, 2 marks are for clarity and communication (correct use of terms, good spelling, and using continuous prose, i.e. avoiding note form). 2 marks are for balance and breadth — good balance of AO1 (knowledge and understanding) and AO2 (evaluation and comment) — as well as addressing more than one way of reducing prejudice. This leaves 4 AO1 marks and 4 AO2 marks. These can be gained in more than one way. For example, two detailed ways of reducing prejudice could gain all 4 AO1 marks. Then you would need to make some criticisms or positive points about them for the AO2 marks. Remember, evaluation points can come from ethical issues, methods used in arriving at the theory or alternative ideas.

Answers to key application questions

(12) Social identity theory claims that prejudice arises when an in-group becomes hostile to an out-group, possibly to enhance the self-esteem of the in-group. ✓ In the source passage, the villagers in each case would probably form an in-group, including not only those who were team members but the whole village. ✓ This would be more likely if one village was seen to be better off than the other, as was the case here. This is an example of scapegoating — where people are blamed for problems they are not responsible for, and prejudice forms. ✓✓ Prejudice can lead to aggression through frustration, and economic disadvantages can lead to frustration. ✓

🖉 Two concepts of how prejudice might occur (SIT and scapegoating) are given here, and each earns 2 marks. In each case, 1 mark is for accurately giving the concept, and 1 mark is for linking well to the passage. A final mark is given for suggesting that frustration might cause the aggression. This links to the frustration–aggression hypothesis, which you may not have studied, and is a good, relevant point from social psychology. Further marks could have been scored by adding that in this case, the villages were in competition but if another situation arose where they had to work together (to solve a superordinate goal, for example), prejudice might be reduced. Ideas from crowd behaviour could also have been used successfully here.

(13) Sherif's (1961) Robber's Cave study involved causing prejudice in two groups of 11-year-old boys. They eventually reduced the prejudice by working together towards a common goal. ✓ (AO1) This cooperation strategy was identified as a way of reducing prejudice, although the drawback with Sherif's study is that the boys had only just developed prejudice, so it may not have been 'real'. ✓ (AO2) Tajfel and Turner developed the social identity theory, and showed that by identi-fying how prejudice can occur, it may be possible to find a way of reducing it. ✓ (AO2) Social identity theory shows that we categorise people as in-group (part of our group) or out-group, and we identify with certain groups, rejecting others. Prejudice occurs when the in-group turns against the out-group. Therefore, not having in-groups and out-groups might help to reduce prejudice. ✓ (AO1)

1 AO1 mark is scored for the Sherif study suggesting that cooperation is useful in reducing prejudice, and 1 mark for the idea that doing away with in-groups and out-groups might also work, even though this is not a very practicable idea. 2 AO2 marks are awarded, 1 mark for saying that investigating how prejudice is formed helps to find ways to reduce it, and 1 mark for saying that the 'prejudice' in the Robber's Cave study might not have been real — in other words, the study may not have been valid. The answer needs more elaboration, for example a discussion about redrawing boundaries or explaining superordinate goals. Alternatively, it could give more ways to reduce prejudice, for example mentioning equal status. As the answer is rather limited in both AO1 and AO2, just 1 balance and breadth mark is awarded. Clarity and communication are fine, and 2 marks are awarded. Note that the explanation for how prejudice is formed does not receive credit. This answer scores 7 marks out of 12.

■ ■ ■

Contemporary issue

(14) **Social psychology can be used to help us understand contemporary issues or debates in psychology. Describe *one* such contemporary issue or debate.** *(4 marks, AO1)*

(15) **Using *two* concepts in social psychology, explain how social psychology can help us to understand the issue or debate that you have outlined above.** *(6 marks, AO2)*

(16) **Use your knowledge of the social approach in psychology to describe and explain *one* contemporary issue or debate.** *(12 marks, essay)*

(14) You need to describe the issue, and give enough material for 4 marks. Try to avoid applying theories. For example, if you are using the issue of the need to reduce prejudice, avoid giving *ways* of reducing it, and describe the *need* for a reduction. Examples might help here. 1 mark is usually awarded for the issue or debate and 3 further marks for saying more about it.

(15) For this part of the question, you need to apply psychology to the issue you have chosen. There are many ways of doing this, and any useful contribution — where you link psychological understanding to the issue, using the right approach — gains marks. You need to say quite a lot for 6 marks, and examples can be useful. You could aim to apply two or three concepts, and earn the other marks by saying more about them.

(16) In this essay question, 2 marks are available for clarity and communication — correct use of terms, good spelling, and using continuous prose (i.e. avoiding note form) — and 2 marks are for balance and breadth. Your answer must have a balance of AO1 (knowledge and understanding) and AO2 (evaluation and comment), as well as describing (very briefly) the contemporary issue and linking concepts to explain it. This leaves 4 AO1 marks and 4 AO2 marks. If the chosen issue is the need to reduce prejudice, the AO1 marks can be gained by giving two or three reasons for prejudice. AO2 marks can be gained by contrasting different explanations or by evaluating how useful they are.

Answers to contemporary issue questions

(14) Football is a sport, but so often there are outbreaks of violence at football matches involving clashes between groups of rival fans. ✓ These clashes often seem to have no personal triggers, but occur as part of group behaviour. ✓

> *e* This is a clear answer, but only gives enough for 2 marks. An example would be useful, as would more detail explaining how information is useful in helping police to control football violence, or to prevent it happening.

(15) One concept is deindividuation. ✓ People do things when they are anonymous that they would not otherwise do. ✓ They get carried away by the behaviour of the crowd around them, and follow the actions of another person. ✓ Ethnocentricity is another concept. ✓ This is the rejection of the out-group and the focus on the in-group. ✓ In a football crowd, the in-group would be the supporters of the team the individual supports, and the out-group would be supporters of the other team. So whatever the in-group is doing, that person would follow, and this would lead to prejudice towards the out-group — and possibly violence. ✓

> *e* Two concepts are chosen well. It is always good to use technical terms, and deindividuation and ethnocentrism are two central issues. A mark is given for each of these. In each case, the answer is elaborated well, for another mark, and then linked to the issue with further expansion. The full 3 marks are awarded for each concept.

(16) Control of crowd behaviour is something that has been investigated in the social approach. In particular, in this country (and others) football crowds have become violent, and this has spoilt enjoyment for many and cost a lot in terms of policing (and injuries). ✓ (AO1) The social approach has shown that people are deindividuated in a crowd and may do things they would not otherwise do. ✓ (AO1) If video cameras are used, or if only season-ticket holders are allowed into the game, then this might avoid deindividuation because individuals could be identified. ✓ (AO1/2) This should help to prevent football hooliganism. Crowds can also be affected by emotional contagion where emotions are caught by those around, and previously calm individuals may become violent. ✓ (AO1) A way of avoiding this is to keep the crowd calm. If people do not all stand together but stadiums are all seating with no standing, this might help to avoid pressure. ✓ (AO1/2) Social psychology studies can be experimental, which means the situation can be unnatural and so not applicable to real life. ✓ (AO2). However, many studies are done in the field as observations, and much can be discovered from these. ✓ (AO2)

e This essay focuses well on the issue. 1 mark is given for the issue and 1 mark for explaining deindividuation. A further mark is awarded, which could be accepted as knowledge and understanding (showing how deindividuation can be combated) or as evaluation and comment (showing how football hooliganism can be avoided). In this case, it could be AO1 or AO2, so both are indicated. Similarly, 1 mark is given for talking about emotional contagion, and then a further AO1 or AO2 mark is allowed for showing how this can be overcome. The final 2 marks are clearly for evaluation, so are AO2 marks. The answer is well expressed, so 2 marks are awarded for clarity and communication. It is also balanced, and so earns 2 marks for balance and breadth. When marks are allocated, the AO1/2 marks are given in the best interest of the candidate, so one is given as AO1 and one as AO2 in this case. A total of 11 marks is awarded. Another mark could have come from mentioning another concept (AO1), such as ethnocentrism (in-group/out-group), or from another comment (AO2), such as how concepts such as formation of prejudice can be used to explain football violence too.

The cognitive-developmental approach

Key assumptions

(1) Outline *one* key assumption of the cognitive-developmental approach.   (3 marks, AO1)

(2) Give *two* key assumptions of the cognitive-developmental approach.   (2 marks, AO1)

(3) In the boxes below, tick the *two* statements that apply to the cognitive-developmental approach.   (2 marks, AO1)

We are guided strongly by our unconscious	☐
A 2-year-old child's ability with regard to thinking is not the same as the ability of an 8-year-old	☐
Information is processed by the brain; there is input, processing and output	☐
Children develop through set stages	☐

> *e* **(1)** Say three things about a key assumption of this approach. 1 mark is likely to be given for knowing the assumption (naming it), and 2 further marks for saying more about it. An example is a useful idea, but keep it short as it will not be worth 2 marks.
>
> **(2)** Here, just naming two key assumptions is fine. You don't have to say more about them.
>
> **(3)** Two ticks are required — no crosses.

Answers to key assumptions questions

(1) It claims that children develop through four different stages, and that everyone goes through the same stages — they are invariant. ✓ However, children at a certain stage might not all be at the same age. ✓

> *e* 1 mark is given for the assumption — that there are invariant stages (which everyone goes through), and another for elaboration by showing that the ages can vary. The answer needs more material for the third mark; for example, not all cognitive-developmental theorists believe that there are four stages.

(2) Children are not the same as adults in that their thinking is qualitatively different. ✓

> *e* This is a good answer, but there is only one assumption here, so only 1 of the 2 marks is awarded.

(3) We are guided strongly by our unconscious   ☐

A 2-year-old child's ability with regard to thinking is not the same as the ability of an 8-year-old   ☑ ✓

Information is processed by the brain; there is input, processing and output ☐
Children develop through set stages ☑ ✓

e The ticks show the correct statements, for 2 marks.

■ ■ ■

Common research methods

(4) Give *one* strength and *one* weakness of observation as a research method.　(4 marks, AO2)
(5) Describe *one* research method commonly used in the cognitive-
developmental approach.　(4 marks, AO1)

e **(4)** There are 2 marks for the strength and 2 marks for the weakness. Don't just give
an answer for each; be sure to expand it enough for the full 2 marks. For example,
say what the strength is, and then say something else to explain it further.

(5) Focus on description, not evaluation, here. If you choose to describe the
observation method, for example, then be sure to describe what takes place.
For example, mention overt and covert observations, what type of data are
gathered, and so on. For this question, do not say what is good and bad about
the method — just say what it is. An example is a good idea, but don't give too
much detail as this would not help to describe the method.

Answers to common research methods questions

(4) One strength is that people are observed doing natural things, so this is a more
valid method than an experiment. When natural settings are used, a study is said
to have ecological validity. If real-life data are being gathered, this is better than
studying artificial behaviour. ✓✓ One weakness is that there might be observer
bias. ✓

e The strength is given clearly but the weakness needs more explanation. The
candidate needs to say *how* there might be bias.

(5) Observations are common. They involve studying people in their natural setting. ✓
The researcher watches and records behaviour. ✓ A tally chart can be used, with
categories for what is to be observed. ✓ Covert observations are when those being
watched do not know about it. ✓

e This is just enough for 4 marks, but more detail would strengthen it. Observations
are commonly used in this approach. They involve a natural setting, so 1 mark is
awarded. Watching and recording behaviour is the main activity, for another mark.
Tallying is mentioned, and is worth an extra mark. More could have been made of
these points. A further point is made about covert observations, for the final mark.

■ ■ ■

section

In-depth area(s) of study

(6) **Match each definition with the appropriate term by drawing a line between them.** (4 marks, AO1)

Term	Definition
Assimilation	A way of organising experience to make the world more predictable
Schema	Applying a schema that already exists, and fitting objects into it
Accommodation	The process of accommodation and assimilation
Adaptation	Changing an existing schema to match requirements of the environment

(7) **What is meant by the term 'egocentric'?** (2 marks, AO1)

(8) **What is meant by the term 'accommodation'?** (2 marks, AO1)

(9) **Describe *one* theory of cognitive development other than Piaget's.** (5 marks, AO1)

(10) **Outline *two* criticisms of a theory of cognitive development other than Piaget's.** (4 marks, AO2)

(6) Draw lines linking the definition and the term. 1 mark is available for each correctly drawn line.

(7) A simple definition will gain 1 mark and a more detailed definition will gain 2 marks.

(8) A simple definition will gain 1 mark and a fuller definition will gain 2 marks.

(9) Giving one theory other than Piaget's is likely to get you the first mark. There are 4 marks for expanding on your answer. Say what the theory is, and make sure you say quite a lot about it — enough for the 4 extra marks. Imagine describing it to a member of your family who has not studied psychology.

(10) 2 marks are available for each criticism. 1 mark will be for stating the criticism, and 1 mark will be for elaboration.

Answers to in-depth areas of study questions

(6)

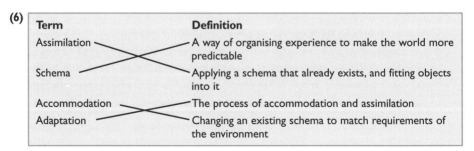

e The correct lines are drawn, for 4 marks.

(7) Children see things from their own point of view. ✓ They do not realise that others have a right to have a different viewpoint.

> e This answer gets 1 mark. The candidate says what egocentric means but does not communicate it clearly. The second part of the answer is incorrect. An example would help to explain what egocentric means, or the first sentence could simply be expanded to explain the term more fully.

(8) Changing an existing schema to accommodate new information. ✓

> e There is no problem with this definition except that it is not enough for the full 2 marks. An example could be given, or accommodation could be contrasted with assimilation to explain it more fully. The definition could be elaborated to explain how accommodation is the way in which new schema are built to avoid disequilibrium.

(9) The three-mountain study showed that younger children are egocentric.

> e This is about a study and not a theory, so no marks are given. Bruner's theory could be described here.

(10) Bruner thought that children went through different modes of representation as they developed, and this is like a stage theory. Behaviourists, though, think that everyone develops continuously, learning all the time, which suggests that the idea of stage-like development is not useful. ✓✓ The age at which different children go through the stages varies in any case, so it is not good at predicting anything, and therefore is not useful. ✓

> e Two criticisms are given. The first is that the idea of stages has been countered by learning theorists. This is awarded 2 marks, as the general idea of the criticism of stages is credited, and then the explanation of the behaviourist view is taken as elaboration. The final criticism scores only 1 mark, as it needs to be linked to Bruner. However, looking at a theory's usefulness is a good way of evaluating it.

■ ■ ■

Two studies

(11) **Describe *one* study from the cognitive-developmental approach.** (5 marks, AO1)

(12) **Evaluate *one* study from the cognitive-developmental approach.** (5 marks, AO2)

(13) **Outline the procedures of two studies from the cognitive-developmental approach.** (6 marks, AO1)

> e **(11)** Note that just describing what was done in the study (the procedure), or what was found (the results or findings), is not enough for all 5 marks. For the first mark, make sure the study is identifiable. 1 mark can be gained for stating the

aim of the study; 2 more marks for saying what was done; and 2 further marks for saying what was found (the results). Marks can also be gained by stating the conclusion. There are more ways than one to get the 5 marks.

(12) Evaluation can come in many forms. You can raise ethical issues (good and/or bad), alternative theories or studies, methodological problems (such as the reliability of experiments or the limitations of case studies) or criticisms of the study itself. Just be sure to write enough for 5 marks. You are trying to say five things, although it is possible to gain more than 1 mark for a well made point.

(13) 3 marks are available for each procedure. Note that you do not have to outline the whole study in the sense of giving an aim, the method, results and a conclusion. You are asked to outline the procedure only in each case. Assume the examiner knows the aim and the results, and just say what was actually done in each of the studies.

Answers to two studies questions

(11) Piaget's three-mountains study ✓ was carried out to see if children in the pre-operational stage could see things from another's point of view, or whether they were egocentric. ✓ A model of three mountains was built, of three different heights; one with a church on top, one with snow and one with a house. ✓ The researchers took pictures of different viewpoints, and let the child walk around the model. Then they placed a doll on one side of the mountain and the child sat on the other side. ✓ The child had to pick the picture that showed the doll's viewpoint.

> 🄴 This is a suitable study and it is described well. 1 mark is given for the study itself, 1 mark for the aim and 2 marks for the procedure. The final mark would have been awarded for stating the results and/or conclusion.

(12) Another study showed that pre-operational children are not egocentric. Using Lego bricks, a policeman doll and another doll, it was shown that children knew where a doll could 'hide' from a policeman — they could take the viewpoint of the policeman. This went against the findings of the mountain task. ✓✓ It was claimed that the mountain task did not make sense to the child, and that is why they could not do it. ✓ The problem with experiments is that they are unnatural, and might not be valid, as shown here. ✓

> 🄴 Using one study to criticise another is useful evaluation. Double marks are given, firstly for briefly explaining the other study, and secondly for making the point that it criticises the findings of the mountain task. Simply describing the other study would not gain marks — the evaluation point must be made. A further mark is needed, and this could be gained by giving another evaluative point. For example, it could be said that in fact the mountain task is well replicated, and is reliable, and so it seems that Piaget did find something out from it.

(13) In the mountain task, a model of three mountains was used, each with a different feature to identify it. ✓ A child was seated on one side of the model and a doll was placed on the other side. ✓ The task was for the child to pick out the picture that represented the doll's view of the mountains. The child was allowed to walk around the model first, to see all the viewpoints. ✓

In Piaget's conservation of liquid task, three containers were used. Two of them were short and wide and the third container was tall and thinner. ✓ Water was poured into the two wider containers until the child realised that there was the same amount of water in each container. Once this was established, the water was poured from one of the short containers into the tall one. ✓ So the child was looking at the water level in the short container and the water level in the tall container. Then they were asked whether there was the same amount of water in both containers, to see if they could conserve volume. ✓

🅮 The procedures of two appropriate studies are clearly outlined for 3 marks each.

■ ■ ■

Key application

(14) Studies and theories within the cognitive-developmental approach have been used in education, usually with a view to improving learning. Discuss the application of the cognitive-developmental approach to education. (12 marks, essay)

🅮 In this essay question, 2 marks are for clarity and communication, gained by correct use of terms, good spelling, and using continuous prose (i.e. avoiding note form). 2 marks are for balance and breadth, gained by giving a good balance of AO1 (knowledge and understanding) and AO2 (evaluation and comment). This leaves 4 AO1 marks and 4 AO2 marks. It would be a good idea to give more than one example of how concepts from the cognitive-developmental approach have been used in education. Avoid describing the theories or studies within the approach, and focus precisely on how they are applied to education. For example, do not outline Piaget's stages but explain how knowing about these stages can help teachers to structure their lessons to suit the cognitive understanding of the child.

Answer to key application question

(14) Both Piaget's and Vygotsky's principles have been applied to education. Piaget had a great influence on the structure of education as a whole. His theory, that we learn at our own rate, led to the customisation of education to the individual. ✓ (AO1) Although each class is set goals to achieve, the teacher now looks at each student, following Piaget's lead. Now there is more flexibility, rather than the old, rigid school structure. ✓ (AO2) Piaget's influence is noticeable in early years too — in pre-school education. The focus has shifted to learning by inter-action. ✓ (AO1) Materials are provided, and creativity is encouraged, reflecting the idea of discovery learning. ✓ (AO1) Vygotsky and Bruner have also influenced education, emphasising how to support the child and accelerate learning.

section

Vygotsky's zone of proximal development can be seen as applied by scaffolding — where the child is allowed to continue a task unaided until a barrier is reached, at which point they are helped and then left alone again to continue. ✓ (AO1, max) Piaget did not look at how to accelerate a child's learning, as he thought that children mature through stages by building upon their own experiences. In this way, Bruner's and Vygotsky's theories differ from Piaget's. ✓ (AO2)

🖉 This is a good essay, and 2 marks each are given for clarity and communication, and for balance and breadth. The focus is on applying theories to education throughout, so the question is answered well. Full marks are given for knowledge and understanding. 2 more marks are needed for evaluation and comment. Mention could be made of how Piaget, unlike Bruner, did not stress the importance of language, or how, as children get older, there may be a case for whole-class teaching rather than the discovery learning advocated.

■ ■ ■

Contemporary issue

(15) Outline *one* contemporary issue or debate that can be explained using the cognitive-developmental approach. (3 marks, AO1)

(16) Explain how the cognitive-developmental approach can help us to understand this issue or debate. (6 marks, AO2)

(17) Use your knowledge of the cognitive-developmental approach in psychology to describe and explain *one* contemporary issue or debate. (10 marks, essay)

🖉 **(15)** You simply need to outline the issue here. You should try to avoid applying theories, but some are hard to separate from issues, for example whether to use cooperative learning or not in education. 1 mark is usually for the issue itself and 2 further marks are available for saying more about it.

(16) For this part of the question, you need to apply psychology to the issue outlined in your answer to question 15. There are many ways of doing this and any useful contribution — where you link psychological understanding to the issue, using the right approach — gains marks. You need to say quite a lot for 6 marks, and examples can be useful. You could aim to apply two or three concepts, and earn the other marks by saying more about them.

(17) In this essay question, 2 marks are available for clarity and communication, gained by correct use of terms, good spelling, and using continuous prose (i.e. avoiding note form). 2 marks are for balance and breadth, gained by giving a good balance of AO1 (knowledge and understanding) and AO2 (evaluation and comment). Be sure to say what the issue is (briefly, this time), as well as to apply theories. This leaves 3 AO1 marks and 3 AO2 marks.

Answers to contemporary issue questions

(15) We focus a great deal on education, and there has been much discussion about whether children learn better individually, or whether they learn best from each other. ✓ Primary schools deliberately set classrooms out in groups for children to work cooperatively. ✓ However, there are times when setting tables out in rows might be more beneficial, so that children can concentrate. ✓ The issue is, which is best? The answer is probably that both can be useful.

> *e* The issue is set out well and there is enough information for the full 3 marks to be awarded. 1 mark is for the issue itself, and 2 more marks are for saying more about it.

(16) With regard to whether children learn best individually, Vygotsky discussed the zone of proximal development and suggested that children learn well if they work within an area of knowledge where they nearly have understanding. ✓ Within that area, they are helped by having others explain things to them. These others can be teachers or peers, and collaborative learning helps. ✓ So, having the room set out with grouped tables is probably useful, as children can learn from one another. ✓ Bruner talks about scaffolding. However, research is mainly done in primary school, so learning for older children might be different. ✓

> *e* This answer focuses well on how Vygotsky advocates collaborative learning, for 3 marks. 1 mark is also given for a rather vague point about research findings being limited to primary school age children. The answer starts to make a useful point about Bruner and scaffolding, but the point is not clearly communicated and needs more explanation, saying what scaffolding is and linking it to the issue. This would have gained the additional marks needed.

(17) Primary schools have set up classrooms so that small groups work together, although in secondary schools rows of desks can still be found. There is a debate between whole-class teaching and group work. ✓ (AO1) Group work seems to be favoured and this reflects evidence from cognitive-developmental studies showing that collaborative learning works well. ✓ (AO1) Vygotsky emphasised how children could help one another. He also focused on the zone of proximal development which is where children find things just outside their ability. ✓ (AO1) Much of this research is done in primary schools, so simply claiming that it is true for older children too may not be justified. ✓ (AO2) From what is said above, for younger children at least, having the room set out in groups of tables is probably useful. ✓ (AO1/2) One good thing about collaborative learning is that both the 'teacher' child and the 'learner' benefit from the experience. It can be seen that research from the cognitive-developmental approach has been used successfully to improve a child's learning experience by suggesting the usefulness of group work. ✓ (AO2) If the zone of proximal development is important, each individual child needs to be challenged, so perhaps individual teaching rather than whole-class teaching is best. ✓ (AO2) On the other hand, whole-class teaching may help children to focus on the task, and may help concentration. The teaching would, however, have to take account of the stage or abilities of the individuals within the class. ✓ (AO2)

e There are a number of different ways of giving marks for this answer, as there are a few comments that are not elaborated but are useful points. As it is clear that this essay will get full marks in any case, there is no need to be precise about which point gets the mark, and an examiner will mentally carry forward possible marks, to allocate total marks fairly. This answer is an example of how that can be done. Also, note that there is one point that could be interpreted as AO1 knowledge and understanding or as AO2 comment and evaluation. The examiner works to give the answer the most credit. Full marks are awarded for clarity and communication and for balance and breadth. There are four AO1 and four AO2 points made, so this essay receives full marks.